HAUNTED FRENCH QUARTER HOTELS

HAUNTED FRENCH QUARTER HOTELS

NICOLE BEAUCHAMP

Published by Haunted America
A division of The History Press
An imprint of Arcadia Publishing
Charleston, SC
www.historypress.com

First published 2025

Manufactured in the United States

ISBN 9781467159357

Library of Congress Control Number: 2025937578

For my New Orleans girl and the love of my life, Alishia Michelle Stagray.

Alishia Michelle Stagray. *Courtesy of Amy Shabluk.*

CONTENTS

FOREWORD

Nicole Beauchamp is a phenomenal writer, a professional paranormal investigator and my friend. I met Nicole, like many up-and-coming authors, when she contacted me to inquire about my books and experiences and to invite me to attend the Michigan Paranormal Convention. Having personally visited hundreds of haunted inns and hotels, I was happy to share my tales with her. From a young age, Nicole was not only captivated by unexplained phenomena, but she also took an active role in exploring strange occurrences firsthand. In 2009, she founded her second and most successful investigative team, Tri-City Ghost Hunters Society—a group she built on her own, which became the foundation of her achievements in the field.

While I'm not a paranormal investigator by any means, I am the former owner of the famous Myrtles Plantation in St. Francisville, Louisiana, widely known as the most haunted house in America. Two decades ago, I authored the popular books *The Myrtles Plantation: The True Story of America's Most Haunted House* and the very first book ever written about haunted inns, *Ghostly Encounters: True Stories of America's Haunted Inns and Hotels*, both published by Warner Books (now Hachette Book Group). I've appeared on *Good Morning America* and *Ripley's Believe It or Not!*; been interviewed by Bryant Gumbel on *The Today Show* and Steve Dunleavy of *A Current Affair*, as well as PBS, NBC Nightly News and TV shows in Australia and Japan; and been featured in *Life* magazine, *Playboy*, *USA Today*, *The Wall Street Journal*, *The National Enquirer* and *The Star*, just to name a few. The Myrtles Plantation was recently featured in an episode of Netflix's no.1–rated series *Files of the Unexplained*, and multiple episodes have been dedicated to it on all the standard ghost shows on television, including *Ghost Hunters* and *Unsolved Mysteries*.

When Nicole approached me years ago about a joint writing venture, I was flattered, but having both read her writing and seen firsthand how she approaches her work, I felt she was selling herself short. She didn't need a coauthor, I thought; she could (and would) become a noted and popular writer herself. I couldn't be prouder of her. Her writing style is candid and chatty. I've had the pleasure of reviewing her first two books. Her style and enthusiasm for each chapter are so evident that you feel like she's talking only to you. Her books are exciting, fun and completely historically accurate, and that is what interested me in getting to know her and helped us to form both a working relationship and, over time, a close friendship.

Today, Nicole has become a celebrity in her own right—a successful author of several books and a recognized expert in the paranormal field. She is a highly sought-after personality, frequently appearing at events, on television and internet shows and in print and online articles. Her reputation extends beyond Michigan and the Midwest: she has fans across the United States, Europe, Australia and the United Kingdom.

When I purchased the Myrtles Plantation years ago, ghosts were not a popular topic, and we struggled to keep the hauntings there quiet, fearing no one would come to spend the night in a haunted inn. When I was writing *Ghostly Encounters*, I had a hard time finding owners who were willing to talk openly about the activity they encountered and would agree to have their establishment included in a book about the paranormal. Things have changed today. It seems hotels are now proud to share their haunted history. As more and more people have become fascinated with ghosts and hauntings, paranormal investigators seem to have popped up everywhere, along with a plethora of books on the topic, some legit and, unfortunately, many not. Nicole is different in that her interest is driven by a deep desire to learn the truth and share that with others. She has a deep commitment to historical analysis and to uncovering the truth—even when that truth runs counter to the popular or widely accepted version of the story, which is often changed or manipulated to beef up the "boos," create a more sensational narrative or drive more tourism. She has no trouble differentiating truth from legend, making calls and asking for the hard facts from others. In doing so, she has established a broad network of friends and experts in the field.

One of the problems with the flood of books on hauntings today is that the majority of them are just reconstituted/regurgitated versions of other printed material and, therefore, redundant. This is not the case with Nicole's books, and each chapter is an exciting recounting of a hotel's story—which at times, thanks to her extensive research, is even more colorful than what was previously known.

When I first met Nicole, we instantly connected over our shared passion for Louisiana and particularly New Orleans. I was rooting for her when she finally first got to go there, and it has since become a second home for her. She's spent many hours soaking up the history, culture, food and, of course, haunts of the magical Crescent City. When Louisiana gets in your blood, it's nearly impossible to get out of its clutches. I know!

—Frances Kermeen

PREFACE

I remember as though it was yesterday watching footage of Hurricane Katrina on the news in late September 2005. The storm had made landfall weeks prior, on August 29, but the grim footage was still being shown—peppered with shots of the catastrophic aftermath, showcasing approximately 80 percent of the city of New Orleans underwater and its residents in a state of desperation for food and drink. As a naïve sixteen-year-old who grew up in Bay City, Michigan, I could not fathom at the time what it would be like to lose everything in a storm of that magnitude. Nonetheless, I felt an immense amount of sympathy for what I was seeing on the television. This news hit even closer to home for me when I saw my father, Harold, a U.S. Marine Corps veteran, who always put on a hard exterior, begin sobbing as his head collapsed into his hands, reeling from post-traumatic stress disorder (PTSD). You see, earlier in the month, my father had gone to New Orleans for the first time ever with the American Red Cross to aid in relief efforts. He did everything from assisting in pulling survivors from waterlogged roads and homes to passing out necessities. Because the demand severely outweighed the supplies available, my father experienced extreme guilt and mental anguish as he stood outside the Superdome passing out the few remaining water bottles in his stockpile, surrounded by thousands of displaced locals, many with fading babies and children, begging for a single drop of clean water to alleviate their ungovernable thirst. In fact, it took almost five years for my father to gather the fortitude to return to the city, and when he did, he took my mother and me with him.

Stranded on their rooftop, survivors face the aftermath of Hurricane Katrina. *Public domain. Photography by Jocelyn Augustino.*

We were not sure what awaited us beyond the Orleans Parish sign. My mother and I had never been, and my father's only experience in the city had been a painful one. However, when we finally arrived, we were astonished in the best way imaginable. Despite the weathered appearance of the Big Easy from centuries of being battered by tropical storms and hurricanes, people danced joyously down the streets to brass bands, greeted each other warmly with smiles and laughed in exultation. In that moment, the resiliency of New Orleanians was apparent. These people do not let anything rain on their parade—and I mean that literally. The friendly nature of the locals and the exhilarating energy of the city itself was intoxicating, and for the first time since Hurricane Katrina made landfall, I saw my dad smile again. His smile grew even larger when he discovered that the paranormal was an integral part of the fabric of New Orleanian culture. My father had always loved the paranormal—a passion we shared since I was a small child. Although my father has since passed, the happy memories of the two of us investigating two haunted hotels and taking a Haunted History Tour will remain with me forever. I can only say thank you, New Orleans, for greeting us so warmly in the face of all the adversity you have been forced to endure. I know you have been through an incredible amount of pain and suffering, and with my book, I want nothing more than to make you proud and represent you in the light that you deserve. I love you now and forever.

ACKNOWLEDGEMENTS

A huge thank-you to Joe Gartrell from The History Press for making my wildest dreams a reality. To my late grandparents Alfred and Evelyn Perry for always inspiring my love of writing, reading and travel. To my mother, Ellen; my brother, Bruce; my Aunt Amy; Aunt Irina; Uncle Rex; Uncle Mike; and cousins Perry, Lauren, Alex, Sasha and Maria for being an incredible family. To my late father, Harold, for introducing me to the joy that is New Orleans. To Alishia Stagray for being the most amazing partner I could have ever asked for. Your help, support, love and encouragement have gotten me through so many days, and I simply could not have done this without you at my side. I love you! To Frances Kermeen for writing *The Myrtles Plantation: The True Story of America's Most Haunted House* and *Ghostly Encounters: True Stories of America's Haunted Inns and Hotels*. These books have inspired me beyond measure, and getting to know you personally in addition to your work has been the cherry on top. Thank you for writing the foreword to this book and always lifting me up in my career. To my beloved friends, chosen family and loyal supporters: Micki and Gregg Stagray, Jacob Stagray and Devin Reeson, Jeremy Stagray and DeMarco Mims, Richard and Christy Reardon, Samantha "Sam" Wilbur, Lexy Freeman and Michelle Jean Blankenship. A heartfelt thanks to my cherished paranormal investigation buddies in Northern Ireland: Micheala Cowdrey, Gary Finlay, Ricky Boyle and Neal McMenamin. To Bobby Jereb and Amy Shabluk (Portraits by Amy Michelle) for being the backbone behind the photos within this project. I love you two! To the former and current staff, guests, historians, archivists, educational faculty, organizations, photographers and individuals who provided me with helpful information and abundant resources for the book: Jacob Walker of New Orleans Portrait Photography; Jennifer Navarre, Johanna Baker, Heather Green and Mary Lou Eichhorn of the Historic New Orleans Collection; Marguerite Roberts, Nicholas Albrecht, Noah Epstein, Erin Vogt and Bryan Block of the Vieux Carré Commission; Amy DeNisco and Christina Bryant of the New Orleans Public Library; Kevin Williams of Tulane University Libraries; Sarah Waits of the Archdiocese of New Orleans; Beryl Hunter of the Office of the Clerk of Civil District Court of Orleans Parish; Karley Frankic of the French Quarter Management District; Kimberley Hefner of the National Black Catholic Congress; Misti Gaither of Louisiana Spirits and *QUEST Talk Show: A Journey Into True Crime & Paranormal*; Eryl John of Ancestry.com; Ginger and Bobby Guitreau of the Haunted Hotel; Herb Leonard Jr. of Phototype Productions; Frank Perez, Mark Ristine, Alison Miller, Lavina Sabnani, Cheryl Bananno, Brenda Gale Butler, Margaret Velazquez, Rod Sadler, Anita Gomez, Henry Figueroa, Cari Roy and Cheyanne Disé.

I want to give a heartfelt thanks to my supporters, social media followers, extended family and online friends who have followed my journey from the beginning and know exactly what writing this book meant to me.

CHAPTER 1

DANCING WITH DEATH

BOURBON ORLEANS HOTEL
717 ORLEANS STREET
NEW ORLEANS, LOUISIANA 70116

When one thinks of La Nouvelle-Orléans, as it was originally called, one might think of the glowing neon lights illuminating Bourbon Street in the darkness, musical ensembles marching down the streets, heavenly Cajun cuisine, extravagant Mardi Gras parades, diverse culture, streets littered with beads, jumbo-sized sugary daiquiris, mysterious voodoo rituals and the astounding number of hauntings that have been reported around the city. This vibrant city, now the largest in Louisiana, began as a settlement founded by French colonizer and colonial governor Jean-Baptiste Le Moyne de Bienville on May 7, 1718. The French Quarter, or Vieux Carré, as it's also known, is the oldest neighborhood within the city and believed to be the most haunted. It is impossible to go anywhere in the Crown Jewel of New Orleans without hearing stories about the unearthly happenings that are just a part of everyday life for the locals.

In May 2009, just prior to starting our official paranormal team, Tri-City Ghost Hunters Society, I, along with my parents and soon-to-be members of the society, Ellen and Harold, decided to travel to what has long been believed to be the "most haunted city in America": New Orleans, Louisiana. As a paranormal enthusiast vacationing in New Orleans for the first time ever, I wanted to take advantage of every opportunity that would allow me to meet the many alleged spirits. Luckily, I did not have to look far.

My parents and I searched for spooky hotels in the Quarter that were within walking distance from the exciting life force that is Bourbon Street (something every first-time visitor should experience at least once) and a far

Above: The neon signs of Bourbon Street. *Courtesy of Carol M. Highsmith's America, Library of Congress, Prints and Photographs Division.*

Left: The sign outside the Bourbon Orleans Hotel. *Courtesy of Jacob Walker, New Orleans Portrait Photography.*

cry from the atmosphere of the sleepy Midwestern city I was born in. We focused our attention on the luxurious Bourbon Orleans Hotel, located right in the heart of the French Quarter.

While reading online about the splendid accommodations that the hotel offered (everything from an outdoor heated saltwater pool to ridiculously comfortable plush bedding), we noticed that the hotel was advertised as being intensely haunted. There was no need to look any further. We immediately gave them a call and informed the soft-spoken front desk agent that we were interested in the history and paranormal happenings on the property.

> *Hey, honey! You're curious about our history? Well, you're talkin' to the right person. Our story begins with the Théâtre d'Orléans, which just means Orleans Theatre in English. It was a fancy establishment with an adjoining ballroom that was designed by esteemed architect Benjamin Henry Boneval Latrobe and built upon our foundation in the early 1810s. Its doors wouldn't open until 1815, after the War of 1812 finally ended. Unfortunately, the following year, it was ravaged by flames in a block fire, which wasn't an uncommon way for theatres to meet their demise in those days. Unwilling to accept the devastation, John Davis, the theatre's impresario, secured a $12,000 loan in 1818 to reconstruct the grand playhouse and its adjacent ballroom back to its former grandeur. Both reopened to the public in November 1819, retaining the original Orleans name. The final project ended up costing a whopping $180,000, about fourteen times more than the initial loan Davis acquired! These locations became the cream of the crop amongst the city's elite. Swanky carnival balls, lavish masquerades and phenomenal French operas were regularly hosted here. The upper crust of New Orleans' high society just couldn't stay away!*
>
> *The property was then sold off to philanthropist John McDonogh in 1849. Sadly, his possession of both properties was relatively short as another fire swept through the area in 1866, causing irreparable damage to the theatre. Luckily, the ballroom remained unscathed and wound up being used for state legislative and First District Court sessions during the early part of the 1870s. The Catholic Church took over the property in 1873, and by 1881, part of it was sold to the Sisters of the Holy Family—one of the first African American Catholic religious orders in our country.*
>
> *In 1891, the nuns purchased the former Orleans Ballroom for $21,000 and converted it into a convent.*

Left: Sisters of the Holy Family in New Orleans, Louisiana, circa 1899. *Courtesy of Du Bois, W.E.B. (William Edward Burghardt), 1868–1963, collector, Library of Congress.*

Opposite: A postcard featuring Orleans Street in 1940, with a glimpse of the convent visible at left. *Courtesy of the Postcard Filing Series (Library of Congress).*

It also housed a relocated school by the name of St. Mary's Academy, which was previously located on Chartres Street. A portion of the original ballroom was renovated to make accommodations for the school.

As the Sisters' order grew, so did their need for more space, and so they continued buying and selling off lots to fit their continuously changing needs, which primarily benefitted the impoverished and disadvantaged. I am hard-pressed to think of every way the property has been utilized over the years off the top of my head because they did so much to help the community. Anyways, we didn't become a hotel until 1964, and during that transformative era, the old convent was demolished. However, there was a big debate back then about whether we should integrate the historic ballroom into the new hotel or tear it down. Thankfully, the powers that be chose to preserve it, and it remains here to this day. I hope that helps give you a better understanding of the history here. It is quite extensive, so my apologies for not knowing more. But to top off our rich history, our staff and guests have reported seeing upwards of twenty different ghosts here! Pretty crazy, right?

I continued to listen intently. She went on:

I haven't witnessed them all, but I did see the full-bodied apparitions of a nun and a wounded Confederate soldier. The soldier's usually seen limping in agony down the hallway on the sixth floor. Occasionally, I have even watched these apparitions pass right through the walls and disappear. One time, I encountered a woman dancing in our historic ballroom. Figuring

ORLEANS ST. N.O.LA.
© C. Bennette Moore.
26.

it was just a guest who had sneaked in, I asked her to leave. She faded into the air right in front of me. I questioned my own sanity, until other staff members told me they see her all the time, usually in the wee hours of the morning. When people do see her, she is floating above the ground. To make matters worse, our housekeepers often find a sizeable bloodstain on the carpet in the ballroom, usually after a large event is held, and scrub it clean only to have it resurface minutes later. Rumor has it that in the nineteenth century, two irascible wealthy men fell in love with the same woman at a quadroon ball that was held on our property and dueled it out until one of those men met his maker. Quadroon balls, along with octoroon balls, were held to showcase free young women of mixed racial ancestry to French suitors. To clarify, quadroons were one-quarter Black, and octoroons were one-eighth. These events demonstrate the unjust racial views of society back then. During these balls, men would choose mistresses in a system called plaçage, where formalized relationships were exchanged for financial support and social status. There is a myth that the mothers of these women negotiated contracts with the male prospects, but this is false and perpetuates a harmful misconception about free women of color.

Admittedly, some think we have a ghost pirate here by the name of Raoul and believe he is responsible for the bloodstain. He was also rumored to have been slain on the property in a sword fight over a woman, but certainly not at a ball! Some of our staff have seen a man they believe to be Raoul getting fresh with our lady guests, much to their displeasure. Anyways, that is the lore behind our reemerging bloodstain in the ballroom and how some believe it got there in the first place.

But if you ask me, there may be another explanation—one rooted in real tragedy. On the night of February 26, 1854, just two days before Mardi Gras, the old Orleans Theatre—then located just steps from this very ballroom—suffered a terrible collapse during a packed vaudeville performance. Years earlier, in an effort to make the space feel airier, the theatre had removed some of its support columns, forcing extra weight onto a low-quality, improperly installed iron beam. When that beam gave way, the top gallery came crashing down onto the crowds below. Two young men lost their lives: Florian Malus, a notary, just twenty-seven years old, and fourteen-year-old Fergus Toledano. Some say their spirits never left. So whether it's the passion of a lover's quarrel, a pirate's ghostly mischief or the sorrow of a forgotten disaster, that bloodstain in the ballroom may carry more history than we ever bargained for.

I was intrigued. "What area of the hotel would you say is the most haunted?"

> *The third and sixth floors are where we get the bulk of reported sightings. Room 644 is believed to be the most haunted room in the entire building. We have had people run out of there screaming and never come back. Some guests have even complained that they felt a slap across the face after cursing in that room! Legend has it that a nun committed suicide in that room back when it was a convent. Naturally, the Sisters of the Holy Family have been reluctant to confirm this, but they also haven't denied it, either. In addition to seeing who I believe to be that same nun in the hallway, I saw the habited figure with my own two eyes right up in that room. I will never forget her nonplussed expression as she stood next to the window, staring directly back at me.*

The fire of passion within my soul began to burn. We *needed* that room!

"Is it available tonight, for one week?" I inquired, almost bursting with excitement.

"Yes ma'am. Would you like to book it?"

I jumped on the opportunity, and within seconds, the most terrifying room in the entire Bourbon Orleans Hotel would be our home for the next week. I could not wait to see for myself if the rumors were true.

Walking up to the entrance of the grand hotel and being greeted by the door attendant, I felt a bit out of place in my baggy T-shirt and beat-up flip-flops. I have since learned through my many travels to the Crescent City that open-toed shoes and Bourbon Street simply do not mix. One should always

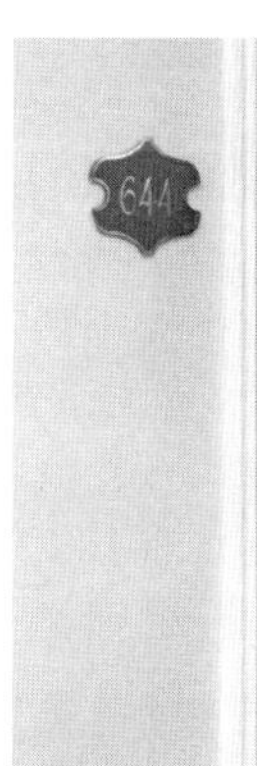

Author Nicole Beauchamp stands in front of the infamous Room 644 at the Bourbon Orleans Hotel, known as the most haunted room in the building and where she stayed on her initial visit to the city. *Courtesy of Amy Shabluk.*

aim to avoid the "Bourbon Street gravy" at all costs, which generally consists of a mixture of vomit, urine, beer, liquor and other suspicious fluids.

As I strolled through the blindingly white front doors of the hotel, I was immediately taken aback by the pure gorgeousness of the lobby. It certainly did not fit the stereotype of what "haunted" is supposed to look like. I felt as if I was in Buckingham Palace awaiting tea with the queen. A sophisticated floral area rug was arrayed across the highly polished marble flooring. The tall ceilings were held up by shiny beams that drew my eye upward to the chandeliers, which looked like sparkling diamonds. A plethora of antique sofas and glossy coffee tables with plants atop made me feel as if I was being enveloped in the beauty of a bygone era. Enthralled, I made my way through the brightly lit lobby to the front desk, where a small, demure lady met us with a welcoming smile.

"Welcome to the Bourbon Orleans Hotel! What can I do for you today?" she asked cheerfully.

"We're checking in. We reserved Room 644."

Her eyes shifted downward to the floor. "You must be the ones who just called."

"Yes, we are."

"This hotel certainly is a sight to behold," the lady said as she forced her focus upward onto the expansive windows that shimmered with the reflected radiance of the glitzy chandeliers. "Despite its beauty," she said as she finally met my eyes, "the reported hauntings are not fictitious. As I mentioned before, I have seen the spirits with my own two eyes. We get all kinds of guest complaints about the screams that come from Room 644, even when it is vacant. Are you sure you'd like to stay there? I would hate for your sleep to be disturbed after a long night out on Bourbon Street." I eagerly reached for the key. With a smile spreading across my face, I replied, "Yes. Yes, I am sure."

My parents and I piled into the elevator with our heavy luggage and took it up to the sixth floor. We wandered down the seemingly infinite hallways adorned with elegant little light fixtures. Finally, we made it to Room 644. It was a posh-looking room with stylish windows, intricately carved wooden headboards, dimly lit lamps and lush forest green carpet. As excited as I was to begin our investigation, it wasn't long after unpacking my toiletries that I fell into a deep sleep. Nothing happened that night.

The next morning, my mother decided she wanted to go for a dip in the pool, while my father went to explore the unique stops within the city. Drinking piña coladas by the vast pool in the courtyard sounded perfect.

I promised I would join my mom for a swim just as soon as I finished changing into my swimsuit. I went into the bathroom and shut the door, just in case my parents forgot something or a member of the housekeeping team came in to straighten up the beds. As I was getting ready, I could hear what sounded like someone enter the room, and I noticed shadows of movement from underneath the door. "Mom? Dad? Is that you?" No response.

I wrapped a towel around myself and peeked my head out from the bathroom door, only to realize that no one was in our room. I thought perhaps it was just simply a play of lights or maybe another guest making noise in an adjacent room, so I shut the bathroom door to finish dressing. I then froze as I heard what sounded like gentle knocking on the bathroom door and lengthy fingernails scraping the surface with each rap. Slowly and quietly, I squatted down and leaned closer, carefully eyeing the gap beneath the door. My vision became fixated on what appeared to be two shiny, distorted-looking black shoes peeking out from what I perceived to be a tunic. I stood in amazement as I watched them slowly pace across the floor as if someone was waiting impatiently for me to exit the bathroom. I pushed my full weight against the door at this point, in an effort to keep out whoever or whatever was out there. I was truly in fear of what awaited me on the other side of the door. At this point, I began to obsess about the idea that there could be a real person out there who had broken into our room and was waiting for me to come out of the bathroom so that they could hurt me. Finally, I stood up and, gathering my strength, flung the door open, only to discover that I was still alone. No one was there.

I hurried down to the pool area where my mom was sunbathing.

"You'll never believe what I just saw!" I exclaimed breathlessly as my mother opened one eye to look at me. "There was someone in our room! I saw their feet under the door when I was in the bathroom, but no one came in and out of the door leading to our room!" My mom initially sat up and looked at me incredulously. However, she could tell by my colorless face that I was not kidding around. Someone or something was in our room, but who and why?

"Are you serious? I would love to experience something like that," she said, as I nodded.

Later, we met my dad for lunch. "Are you absolutely sure that someone from the housekeeping team didn't come into the room, notice that you were in the bathroom and decide to leave and come back at a later time?" he asked inquisitively.

"I promise!" I exclaimed. "It was seconds after I saw the feet that I opened the door. No one was there. Besides, the shoes did not look right. There was something very off about them—they appeared grainy and out of focus."

My father glanced at me sideways before taking a large bite of his jambalaya and arrogantly stated, "Well, when I see it myself, I'll believe it."

I know my dad trusted me implicitly, and deep down, I knew, he believed me—but because the strange experience happened to me and not him, it was hard for him to accept. And truthfully, he was jealous. He so desperately wanted to witness a spirit. My mother and I shared similar views in that if we did not have a ghostly encounter during our stay, we would be totally fine with it. After all, ghosts don't come out on demand.

The following evening, after we got back to the hotel, I wanted to go exploring on my own. I decided to go walking around the property with my camera and document any occurrences that happened. My mom felt pretty tired after a night out on the town, and my dad was dead set on seeing the otherworldly figure that had been roaming around our room just yesterday.

I installed two fresh batteries in my digital point-and-shoot camera prior to taking off on a solo adventure to explore this haunted locale. As I walked through the lengthy hallways, I carefully studied each area that I passed, documenting everything I was seeing via video in case something were to manifest. I kept my eyes peeled for the ghost of the hobbling Confederate soldier and the womanizing buccaneer but never managed to catch a glimpse of either of them. I made my way down to the second floor and admired the exquisite construction of the hotel. I came to the end of a hallway, where ballroom doors beckoned me to enter. I so desired to see the phantom dancer in action, spinning elegantly in the air in her Cinderella-esque ball gown. As I reached for the door in eager anticipation, I heard the bloodcurdling cries of a child behind me. Startled, I whipped around, letting the camera fall to my side as I tried to determine where the sound was coming from.

The child's heart-wrenching sobs were so loud that I found it hard to believe other guests weren't coming out of their rooms and staff weren't coming up to see what was going on. As I started down the hallway, the eerie cries ended abruptly. Noticing one of the hotel room doors was cracked open ever so slightly, I knocked on it, and no one responded. I stood back, and to my horror, the solid wooden door began to open by itself, revealing a dark and empty room. Suddenly, the hysterical child began crying again—only this time, the sound was coming from every room in the hallway. I stood frozen, looking into the dark hotel room, not knowing what exactly I was expected to do. I quickly grabbed the door handle and closed it. As the door banged shut, the deafening sounds of crying that seemed to echo off the walls suddenly became silent. I looked around, bewildered, wondering what the hell was going on, and I heard laughter. It was not just any laughter. It was the sound of a mischievous child who was playing a prank. I ran back to the ballroom doors and crouched down in front of them, hoping to get a full view of anything happening down the hallway.

The lights began to flicker, leaving me in almost complete darkness, as the distinctive laughter of a toddler echoed down the shadowy corridor. Through the darkness, I could make out a tiny girl with light hair wearing a white dress. She was about four years old. Her button nose was red, and her cheeks were stained with tears. As I reached for my camera to catch her on video, she ran into the ladies' bathroom next to where I was standing. I went in after her but could find no trace of her. She was gone.

I stood in place for a moment, processing what I had just witnessed. Was this a real child? If so, where did she go? Or perhaps she was not real at all. Maybe she was playing an infinite game of hide and seek with me. I called out to her, but she did not respond. What if she was lost? I sprinted back to Room 644 to share what had happened with my parents. I burst into the room, urging, "Come on! We must go to the ballroom! There's a child over there!"

"What do you mean, 'There's a child over there'?" my dad asked, concerned.

"Come on, hurry! I'll show you!"

My parents and I stood by the ballroom doors as I explained what took place just minutes ago. I was acting out the scenario when we all heard dated music coming from the ballroom. I felt a jolt as my hand touched the ballroom doors. As we entered, I could sense that we were not alone. We sat on the gigantic ballroom floor and invited the spirits to join us in conversation, inquiring about their names, the year they remained in and their most beloved interests. The only lighting in the room came from the streetlights outside. Listening intently, we could hear the faint sound of classical music filling the air. In the dim light, we could almost make out the milky shape of a woman spinning around across the room. We sat and watched her performance, completely awestruck, until finally she faded away into the night. By this time, we were so enervated that we headed back to our hotel room, but my dad's eyes shone like a lit-up Christmas tree the entire way back.

Taxed from elation, my dad fell fast asleep as my mom and I lay, almost comatose, in bed. I asked my mom if she could please turn the lamp off.

As she reached over, about to flip the switch, the room was suddenly thrust into darkness.

"That wasn't me who did that," she whispered, in shock.

"What do you mean?" I asked.

"My hand didn't even touch the light!"

Okay, I thought. *Two can play this game.* I got out of bed, turned the lamp on and firmly requested, "If someone is here with us, please shut the lamp off." Just as requested, the lamp shut off with no one touching it. "Turn the lamp on, please. I cannot see!" I shouted. A second later, the lamp turned on. Every time my mother and I asked for the lamp to turn on or off, it did so on command. Each time, the toggle switch physically moved back and forth. My mother and I continued doing this until we passed out from complete exhaustion.

In the morning, we again asked that the lamp be turned on, and it was. This time, my dad witnessed the activity. He thought perhaps there was an electrical issue, but even if that were the case, how do you explain why the toggle switch moved, especially when nobody was near it? It is little, unexplainable things like this that make paranormal investigation so suspenseful and unpredictable. For the remainder of our stay, nothing more paranormal occurred, but I was thrilled our stay had been so remarkable early on.

After checkout, as we were leaving, I stood outside, staring up at the glorious building and reflecting on the many experiences we had within its walls. I pulled out my camera and was about to snap a photo when an eccentric older lady approached me. I later learned her name was Ester.

"Well, she sure is a beauty, ain't she?" Ester said, smiling and nodding toward the majestic hotel.

I smiled back. "It's a gorgeous place! We've really enjoyed our stay here. I don't even want to leave!" I replied.

Ester leaned in closer to me. "I meant the little girl in the window, wearing that pretty white dress. Don't you see her?"

The smile quickly faded from my face as I looked eagerly at the windows for a glimpse of the playful yet tormented little girl. Ester said,

> *Well, baby, I've been in New Orleans my whole life, and Catholic nuns used to own this land. I remember walking by and seeing that little girl in the windows of the old convent back when I was just a child. You see, the nuns had opened an orphanage on these grounds in 1892, and they called it St. John Berchman's Orphan Asylum. If y'all used the swimming pool*

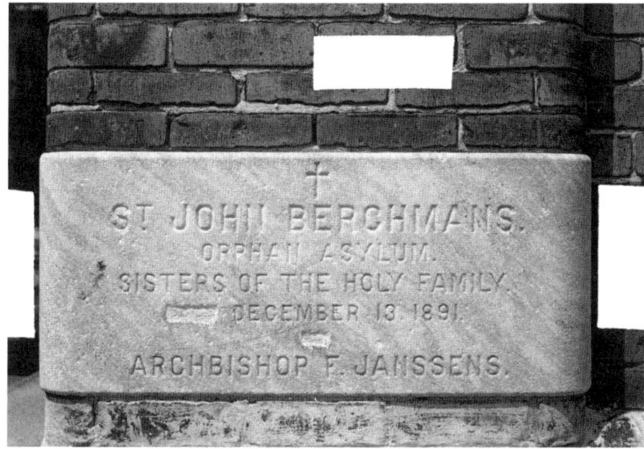

St. John Berchmans Orphan Asylum, once run by the Sisters of the Holy Family, had its cornerstone at 733 Orleans Street, with the primary address at 717–737 Orleans Street. *Courtesy of the Collins C. Diboll Vieux Carré Digital Survey, a project of the Historic New Orleans Collection.*

> *or courtyard during your stay, you may not have realized, but that used to be the very playground and courtyard for the children's home. Those nuns cared for victims of the yellow fever epidemic, and Lord, let me tell you—that epidemic came in recurring waves and sure did last a long time! It started all the way back in 1796—long before the nuns acquired the property—and ended shortly after the turn of the century in 1905. After tens of thousands of people died when the epidemic swept across the city, New Orleans had garnered a real nasty nickname: Necropolis, which means the City of the Dead. A significant reason the orphanage opened in the first place was to take in kids that lost their homes and parents due to disease. The need for housing orphans was so high the city couldn't keep up. I always wondered if that poor lost soul was a victim of the fever. Bless her little heart and all the others who had to die like that.*

My heart began to race as my adrenaline spiked. Suddenly, it all made sense—the child, the voices. As Ester walked off into the distance, my eyes fixated on a jazz musician who was passionately playing his saxophone on a nearby corner, totally immersed in the melody. New Orleans can best be described as a city that continuously celebrates life, despite so much death. With locals like Ester and the front desk agent sharing the stories of those who lived, it's safe to say no one ever really dies here—at least not in spirit.

CHAPTER 2
MUSIC, MADAMS AND MYSTERY

HOTEL VILLA CONVENTO
616 URSULINES AVENUE
NEW ORLEANS, LOUISIANA 70116

Many years ago, a couple decided to book a romantic getaway at Hotel Villa Convento. Shortly after checking in and settling into Room 301, they lay spooning naked in bed, their sexual desires growing more fervent with every little move they made. As the man tenderly brushed his fingertips across his wife's sensitive thighs, the pair was unable to withstand their irrepressible urges any longer. They feverishly locked lips as their bodies intertwined, making love until finally reaching the crescendo of their rapture, which left them lying breathless in the aftermath of passion. Their pleasurable encounter was quickly halted when the man rolled over and his eyes became mirrors of dread, reflecting the horrific sight he was witnessing. Standing at his bedside was a gaunt woman in all-black period dress. Her vacant eyes fixated on him from within her deeply sunken eye sockets. The man's heart began furiously hammering against his ribcage as her cold stare bored directly through his soul. Startled by what he was seeing, the man let out a yell and leapt off the bed, raising his fists as the figure dematerialized in a cloud of darkness. Alarmed, the wife rushed over to her husband to comfort him.

"What's wrong, sweetheart? Are you okay?" she asked, bewildered by his sudden outburst. The man signaled, wide-eyed, to the precise place he'd seen the apparition only moments prior.

Totally aghast, he choked out the words, "Didn't you see her?"

"See who?" his wife asked apprehensively, rubbing his back to soothe him.

Panic-stricken, he cried out, "The lady in black!"

The sign outside the Hotel Villa Convento. *Courtesy of Amy Shabluk.*

The concern on his wife's face began to grow as she shook her head no and held her husband close to her. Her eyes frantically darted around the room in a state of self-preservation, paranoid at the idea of seeing whatever her husband saw.

Throughout the rest of their stay, the couple endured turmoil as they repeatedly heard banging on their hotel room door at regular intervals, which led to arguments over who was doing it and why it was happening. Things became even more strained when the man began hearing catcalls from various female voices during moments of vulnerability, such as while changing, using the bathroom or showering. The sultry whispers in his ears, along with the incessant knocking, filled him with intense trepidation, as he greatly feared that the ghoulish woman would return to his room. These experiences left him unsettled and hypervigilant, eventually leading to his wife questioning his sanity.

After the man recalled his horrifying encounter to a staff member at the front desk, he was regaled with tales of other men who had stayed in Room 301 and reported similar experiences. Apparently, their wives and girlfriends never saw the enigmatic woman either, as her presence seemed to appear only to men. The numerous stories of paranormal encounters began spreading across the country like wildfire, leading ghost hunters and paranormal enthusiasts to flock to the hotel and leaving them questioning who these spirits were and what association they had with the property. To unravel the enigma behind these restless souls, we must first delve into the backstory of one of the most timeless pieces of music in history, as that's where our story begins.

Since June 1964, everyone and their brother has been mindlessly singing along to the Animals' no. 1 hit "House of the Rising Sun" without truly paying attention to its demoralizing lyrics or haunting, hidden meaning. If you find yourself among those who haven't fully grasped the harrowing undertones of the song or its potential origins, don't feel bad, because even Alan Lomax, a famous American ethnomusicologist of the twentieth century, struggled with the same thing.

The classic folk ballad existed long before the Animals ever recorded it, yet they were the ones responsible for catapulting it into popular culture with their commercialized version. Music scholars are convinced that the song predates even the city of New Orleans itself. Over the years, countless variations have emerged, subtly but surely altering the originally intended meaning of the song. Adding to its mystique, connections to the song's title have been discovered worldwide, especially throughout the United Kingdom and Europe. Alan Price of the Animals even once made the claim that the song was written during the Middle Ages about a bordello in Soho, a district in the West End of London. There are various theories about how the associated house in the song traveled across continents only to wind up in New Orleans; Lomax speculated that White Southern entertainers adapted its lyrics to the cities in which they were performing.

In 1925, folklorist Robert Winslow Gordon penned a column in *Adventure Magazine*, which was the first time that the song's lyrics appeared in print. This article attributed the house's location to New Orleans and portrayed the house as "the ruin of many a poor girl." The first known recording of the song came later, in 1933, when Appalachian artists Clarence "Tom" Ashley and Gwen Foster performed their rendition of the song, "Rising House Blues," under the Vocalion label. In this recording, the house is described as "the ruin of many a poor boy," which was how Ashley learned it from his grandfather. Throughout history, female singers have preferred to stick to the originally published lyrics when performing the song.

Historians who have studied the song believe that "the House of the Rising Sun" is a euphemism for a bordello and have surmised, on the basis of that claim, that the song was written about sexual slavery. But did such an establishment actually exist in New Orleans? And if it did, where exactly in the city was it located?

"House of the Rising Sun" is one of the most popular songs covered both vocally and instrumentally by French Quarter musicians, like this guitarist. *Courtesy of Carol M. Highsmith's America, Library of Congress, Prints and Photographs Division.*

In 1821, the *Louisiana Gazette* ran an advertisement by L.S. Hotchkiss and Co. for what was to be a short-lived establishment called Rising Sun Hotel on Conti Street. The ad featured potentially suggestive wording, such as, "Gentlemen may here rely upon finding attentive servants." Archaeological excavations conducted in 2005 at 535–537 Conti Street, where the Rising Sun Hotel once stood, uncovered evidence of many boarding rooms and hotels dating to the late eighteenth and early nineteenth centuries. Items like tin-enameled rouge pots, wine bottles and jewelry were found. While this doesn't prove that the Rising Sun Hotel or any of the other businesses on the site were used specifically as cathouses, it certainly leads to more questions than answers. The existence of businesses with similar names, such as the Rising Sun Coffee House, situated on what is now Decatur Street in the 1860s, and a Rising Sun Hall in the uptown Carrollton neighborhood during the late nineteenth century, further deepen the mystery. Between 1862 and 1874, a madam by the name of Marianne LeSoleil Levant, whose French last name literally translates to "the rising sun" in English, managed two brothels in the city, one at 1614 Esplanade Avenue and the other at 826–830 St. Louis Street. Even the Orleans Parish women's prison featured a carved rising sun on the lintel of its stone entrance. As you can see, the name was associated with various establishments, so the location of the original House of the Rising Sun, if there was just one, remains inconclusive.

Evidence tends to suggest that there were several Houses of the Rising Sun, as studies continue to support the idea that an underground network of brothels was created to evade the law. Houses of ill repute were frequently shut down on discovery, so many brothel keepers got creative to keep the funds flowing.

However, ask Dolly Parton where the House of the Rising Sun is, and she seems to have a solid answer. On November 17, 1980, RCA Records launched Dolly Parton's twenty-third solo studio album, *9 to 5 and Odd Jobs*, which includes a remake of the song. The remake features blunt lyrics depicting the demeaning toil of a working girl in the French Quarter. The lyrics go as follows:

There is a house in New Orleans
Down in the Vieux Carré
A house they call the Rising Sun
Where love and money are made
My father, he was a gambler
Mother died when I was young

And I've worked since then to pleasure the men
At the House of the Rising Sun
There is a house in New Orleans
They call the Rising Sun
It's been the ruin of many a good girl
And oh God, you know I'm one
So mothers, you go telling all your daughters
Not to do what I have done
To live a life of sin, shame and strife
In the House of the Rising Sun
There is a house down in New Orleans
They call the Rising Sun
It's been the ruin of many a good girl
And oh God, you know I'm one
Oh God, you know I'm one

Many music researchers are adamant that Dolly's rendition most accurately conveys what is believed to be the song's original intended meaning; others have chalked the lyrics up to just being lyrics. However, it is widely assumed that these lyrics may hold some historical truth at Hotel Villa Convento. The hotel is located only blocks away from where the bustling French Market stands, formerly home to Gallatin Street, one of the city's first and most dangerous vice districts of the nineteenth century. The area was depicted in a 1938 *Times-Picayune* article as "the street where shadowy forms darted in and out, a lane of sinister doing [where] seamen were 'Shanghaied,' smuggled goods were hidden, and men and women were murdered."

But just as the song's origins are murky, so is a portion of Hotel Villa Convento's history. Most people strongly believe that the building housing the hotel was indeed used at one time as a brothel. However, this area of the city didn't always have that seedy association and, in fact, had rather tame beginnings.

Stand on one of the hotel's balconies and look across the street to your right, and you'll have an overhead view of the Old Ursuline Convent. Constructed between 1745 and 1750, the convent stands not only as one of the oldest structures in the entire Mississippi Valley but also as the finest publicly accessible display of French colonial architecture in the whole United States. Its location is relevant to Hotel Villa Convento's history, as Ursuline nuns once occupied this area during the early days of French colonization.

The French Market circa 1906. *Courtesy of Library of Congress, Prints & Photographs Division, Detroit Publishing Company Collection.*

Governor Bienville, with his connections to Normandy, needed nurses to staff the local military hospital. He called on Father de Beaubois, a French Jesuit priest, to help with the task of finding Sisters to fulfill the role. The Ursuline nuns had previously educated members of Beaubois's family and had an impeccable reputation, so they seemed like the perfect fit. Beaubois would go on to an extend a warm invitation to the Ursuline nuns of Rouen, France, to relocate to New Orleans and establish their order in the colony.

Twelve Sisters from the order arrived in 1727 but didn't have an official convent at which to stay, so they initially were housed in a structure on Chartres Street, which has since been razed. By 1734, their first convent had been completed on the current site of the Old Ursuline Convent complex, though it was situated closer to the river, in what is now the back courtyard of the convent. Their three-story half-timbered building was located right next door to the military hospital, conveniently allowing seamless transitions between both facilities. Unfortunately, the building was no match for the humid subtropical climate, and the structure began rapidly deteriorating. Realizing the urgent need for a more durable structure, the nuns procured funds and had their second convent, a much sturdier building, erected in its place. By the winter of 1751–52, the new convent had been completed, and the nuns reveled with delight.

On August 20, 1805, in recognition of all the social services the Sisters provided to the community, including medical care, education of all free female youth and housing of orphans, the Ursuline nuns were granted land by Colonel Joseph Deville Degoutin Bellechase, a militia officer and city councilman. Almost fourteen years later, land along Ursulines Avenue was subdivided, and parcels of it were sold off to private owners. The first buyer was a prosperous shipbuilder by the name of Arnaud Magnon, who scooped up a portion of the land in the spring of 1819.

Almost a decade after losing her cherished husband, Jean-Baptiste, in 1824, Elizabeth "Lize" Forstall Poeyfarre sought land to build a home that would be wholly hers. Magnon had passed away a few years prior to Jean-Baptiste, in 1821, and by 1833, his widow, Henriette, was selling off the land that would later host 616 Ursulines Avenue. Lize soon learned of this available property and was quick to act, becoming its rightful owner in June that same year. Shortly after acquiring the estate, she commissioned a stunning Greek Revival townhouse on the lot, which stood complete by 1840. After Lize passed in 1845, the home changed hands multiple times before the Taormina family moved in in 1902. The home remained in their possession until 1946, and it's during their period of ownership that the townhouse is believed to have gained its infamous reputation as a makeshift brothel.

After the Civil War ended, much of the South underwent a financial depression. These circumstances fueled a rise in vice as people desperately tried to recover what they had lost. Large numbers of men were seen passing through the doors of the Taormina family home at all hours of the day and night, and whispers began to circulate around town that it was being used as a den of iniquity. Some folks insisted it was nothing more than an innocent dwelling where the family was welcoming company, while others scoffed in disgust, convinced that the Taormina family was enriching themselves on the literal backs of working girls. After all, the geographical location of New Orleans and its working port were ideal for allowing innumerable amounts of lustful men to pass through the city under the radar.

Documentation provided by the Historic New Orleans Collection shows just how rampant prostitution and its associated violence were throughout the city in the late 1800s—so much so that Alderman Sidney Story proposed a city ordinance in 1897 to set up a red-light district to regulate illicit acts and contain where they were happening. The district became known as Storyville and quickly gained the reputation of the nation's most notorious red-light district for its explicit depravity. Men traveled far and wide to meet the ladies of the night and fulfill their every perverted desire, and thus the insatiable appetite for paid sex flourished. An influx of unauthorized brothels popped up across the city to help satisfy the ever-growing demand. Storyville was finally shut down in 1917, but as I'm sure you know, to this day, prostitution remains a thriving industry. We can't say for certain that the present-day Hotel Villa Convento was ever used as a bordello, but we also can't say that it wasn't, because even places that operated within the Storyville limits and were obviously brothels were still vague in the paper trails they left behind. For example, in historical documentation, these establishments were marked with an "FB," which means "female boarding"—but that doesn't account for any of the other properties used for male "entertainment" that operated outside of the confines of Storyville.

In early 1946, the American General Savings and Loan Association obtained the Taormina home, which went on to see a series of new owners as the years went by. The property was transformed into a multi-tenant house called the Old Town Villa, where American singer-songwriter Jimmy Buffett resided in apartment 305. Later, during the early 1970s, the rooming house would be repurposed into the hotel we now know it as. In 1983, the property was purchased for the last time, by the Campo family, whose ancestors settled in New Orleans from the Canary Islands in the late eighteenth century. Today, members of the family proudly own and operate Hotel Villa Convento, embracing the property's historically controversial label as the House of the Rising Sun—and they've heard their fair share of ghost stories, too.

The cadaverous woman in black who appeared at the beginning of this chapter is Hotel Villa Convento's resident spirit, known by staff and guests alike as the Madam. Her ghost lingers from the hotel's purported bordello days, forever bound within its corridors. Many believe that her ghost exhibits both intelligent and residual characteristics: intelligent in that she's always aware of who's entering and exiting the property but residual in that every twenty minutes, she makes her rounds to knock on guests' doors, letting the men know their time is up. Though seemingly harmless, her presence evokes unbridled terror in even the most courageous of men.

The spectral ladies who work under the Madam, however, do not discriminate in who they appear to and often are responsible for causing quite a ruckus throughout the property. In the late hours of the night and

A Storyville woman enjoying a glass of Raleigh Rye whiskey. *Courtesy of the Historic New Orleans Collection, 1981.177.9.*

the wee hours of the morning, guests are rudely awakened by a cacophony of pleasure emanating from an adjacent room: the undeniable sounds of a headboard slamming against the wall rumble like thunder in the stillness of night, as flirtatious giggles and unrestrained moaning rise and fall like the tide. Often, this sexual symphony gets so loud that guests get up to investigate where the sounds are coming from and shout at who they believe to be the neighboring guests to quiet down so they can sleep. Although these sorts of sounds aren't at all unusual to hear in a hotel, whenever guests report these boisterous occurrences to staff in the morning, they're informed that the rooms the sounds originated from were either unoccupied or under construction.

It appears that this hotel is so riddled with entities that no matter what room you're assigned, you're bound to have some sort of spine-tingling experience. Some rooms are naturally more active than others, and in other cases, the ghosts are just waiting for the right time to emerge.

Lavina Sabnani, a resident of Hong Kong, stayed the night alone on the property for the first (and last) time in the summer of 2021. At the time, she was pursuing her graduate degree from Georgetown University in Washington, D.C., and decided to take a little trip to New Orleans for a few nights of fun.

On the last day of her trip, Lavina's flight was delayed by a full twenty-four hours, and she sought an affordable place where she could rest her head and shower. While doing an internet search, she came across Hotel Villa Convento and was enticed by its quintessential French Quarter appearance: its charming redbrick façade, muted forest green shutters and black wrought iron railings. When Lavina arrived on-site, her room wasn't quite ready yet, so she dropped her luggage off and went out exploring before retiring to her room in the evening. Although she couldn't recall specifically which room number she stayed in, Lavina described it as being on an upper floor near the staircase. She stated that on entering the room, even though it had two windows, it seemed ominously dark, and the energy within the room felt amiss. Despite her feelings of unease, Lavina continued as though everything was fine and began unpacking her toiletries atop a dresser.

While putting down the last product, she caught a glimpse of herself in the mirror on the dresser and realized, much to her horror, that an opaque shadow figure loomed against the wall behind her, its silhouette darker than the midnight sky. Lavina couldn't believe what she was seeing as the figure's abyssal black eyes met with hers in the reflection. Letting out an audible gasp, she whipped around in fright but saw nothing standing behind her. It was quite late, and all the staff had gone home for the night, so Lavina knew she had no choice but to tough it out until morning. Putting on music to attempt to quiet her racing mind, she thought the warm, cascading water of a shower might help her relax further.

While showering, Lavina began to sense that she was no longer alone in the bathroom and quickly finished up so she could get out of there and go text her partner from the comfort of the bed. On getting into bed, she could see what looked like dark figures passing repeatedly in front of the windows of her upper-story room, but these sights were never accompanied by any noise. Lavina was relieved when, suddenly, she heard rhythmic knocking on her door, hoping it was an employee who could put her in a different room. But when she swung the door open, she saw that the hallway remained free of life. Two knocks came later, with time between each, suggesting that perhaps the Madam was in residual mode.

The last straw came when Lavina, who was having trouble sleeping, finally drifted off at three o'clock in the morning, only to be jarred awake by a phantom hand tapping her on the shoulder. At this point, Lavina was too horrified to sleep, and she turned on every light in the room. To once again settle her nerves, she began watching Netflix on her laptop as she clutched her om necklace, a symbol of spiritual well-being, tightly in her hands. When the sun came up about four hours later, Lavina vacated the premises, with no desire to ever return and relive what she went through. "I'm not a ghost hunter or someone who seeks this stuff out. I was just a normal person who was hanging out with friends and partying in New Orleans. That experience scared the hell out of me," Lavina said of the encounter, which left her shaken to the bone.

Alison Miller, on the other hand, had a somewhat similar encounter to Lavina in the shower and yet willingly comes back to the property year after year. Alison has been a regular guest of the hotel for over a decade; she was introduced to it for the very first time while taking a trip with some friends. Her first paranormal encounter happened in a second-floor balcony room when the door swung rapidly open of its own accord, stopping right before it struck the wall. This minor incident couldn't keep her away from Hotel Villa Convento's old-world charm, and she eventually brought her husband there on subsequent visits, staying in various rooms over the years, including suites on the upper floor. But it was in Room 400, a suite on the top floor, where things finally took a perturbing turn for her. Room 401 didn't appear to have much activity, but Room 400 was a whole different story.

One incident occurred when Alison was getting ready to start her day and headed to the bathroom to take a shower. As she made her way there, she couldn't help but notice that an unusual orb with a misty appearance darted through the door ahead of her. After entering the seemingly empty bathroom, she got undressed, stepped into the shower and turned the water on. A feeling of unease came over her. She sensed a presence, as though someone had entered the room. Thinking it was her husband, she peeked out from behind the curtain, but he wasn't in there. Closing the curtain to start washing up, she heard a loud *tsk* in her ear that sent a chill straight through her core.

Later that evening, after Alison and her husband fell fast asleep, they were awakened to their bed shaking. In total disbelief at what was happening, they tried to rationalize the bizarre occurrence, but in the moment, it was a bit overwhelming. They later learned the rattling could have been from a heavy cargo truck passing through the Quarter, but after Alison's experience in the bathroom, she couldn't shake the feeling that something supernatural was at play. But unlike the next guest, Alison desires to keep coming back, hoping to one day unravel the mystery about what lies beyond.

One annual guest of Room 302 found comfort there for years until she bore witness to an unexpected ghostly manifestation and refuses to ever come back to the property. One night, as she lay resting peacefully in bed, a humanoid form materialized in plain sight, paralyzing her into a state of shock. She kept the details of the encounter close to her heart, never sharing the full extent of what she saw that night. What do you suppose dwells within Room 302? One may never know without enduring a full night's stay.

Meanwhile, an intensely chilling aura emanates from the Jimmy Buffett Room, Room 305—a room employees avoid entering unless they absolutely must. Lastly, the hotel's most notorious room remains difficult to enter *and* difficult to book, standing as a chilling testament to a harrowing event from the building's past as a multi-tenant house in the mid-twentieth century.

Room 209 was once home to thirty-eight-year-old George J. Engloff, a talented artist and poet who once worked in the French Quarter. In October 1968, he fell into an unescapable depression after learning he might have kidney cancer. In a state of hopelessness, he filled the tub with water, got inside and took matters into his own hands before he could succumb to his potential disease. The next morning, Cassie Barton, his landlady, went to wake him up for his scheduled admittance to the hospital and became hysterical on finding his bloated body. Since then, his disturbed presence manifests through distressing disembodied voices, heartfelt sobs and poltergeist-like behavior: guests' belongings get carelessly strewn about, as Engloff doesn't seem too keen on strangers staying in his former residence. This room is widely regarded as the hotel's most haunted, evoking feelings of despair and emptiness in anyone who dares to enter.

Skepticism surrounding Hotel Villa Convento's alleged past persists to this day, but one thing is undeniable: this property has proven time and time again to be a portal to the other side. Whether you're a paranormal enthusiast, someone who just likes a thrill or a fan of the song "House of the Rising Sun," Hotel Villa Convento is *the* place to stay, as staff members welcome you with open arms and spirits welcome you with unseen eyes. You'll never get bored trying to discover what secrets remain locked within these walls. If you're brave enough to last an entire night in one of the hotel's most haunted rooms, perhaps you'll come face to face with the Madam, a spectral lady of the night, a looming pitch-black shadow figure, the melancholic Mr. Engloff or someone else who has yet to manifest—the possibilities are endless. Do you have what it takes to last the night?

CHAPTER 3
SPECTERS OF THE SCARLET GLOW

DAUPHINE ORLEANS HOTEL
415 DAUPHINE STREET
NEW ORLEANS, LOUISIANA 70112

Just a brief jaunt away from the vivacious spirit of Bourbon Street sits the Dauphine Orleans Hotel, an elegant retreat made up of an assemblage of storied buildings. Entwined with the historic architecture of this boutique hotel lies a realm where the past and present converge, and spirited beings wander forevermore. Throughout the wide grounds, both visitors and employees have reported a plethora of spooky happenings. These range from sleepless nights disturbed by the heavy tread of marching boots to sightings of various apparitions linked to the property's multifaceted and checkered past.

Throughout its history, since the United States' birth, the land encompassing 409–425 Dauphine Street, now consolidated as 415 Dauphine, has witnessed constant transformation. For over two centuries, the land has served myriad purposes, and the structures across the plots have endured erection, demolition, relocation and renovation, each change contributing to the legacy of this haunted locale.

In the late 1780s, a portion of the land was owned by Don Andrés Almonaster y Roxas, a real estate magnate who played a pivotal role in the city's development. Recognizing the urgent need for health care amid rampant disease in the bustling port town of New Orleans, the property tycoon generously donated what he owned of the land to Charity Hospital. Unfortunately, the exact use of the land during that period remains unclear due to limited historical records.

During and after the French and Spanish governance eras, ownership of different parcels of the land shifted among business figures, free people of color and families of high social status such as the Chauvins, Macartys, Broutins, Trepagniers and Bonabels.

From 1821 to 1822, the renowned French American ornithologist, naturalist and painter John James Audubon briefly resided at 509 Dauphine Street (now the Audubon Cottages). Adjacent to his former home, at the intersection of Dauphine and Conti Streets, he worked in a Creole cottage that served as his art studio, and the room where he completed several of his iconic *Birds of America* paintings is now known as the Audubon Room. This cottage, built prior to 1813, has since been incorporated as an extension of the hotel bar, May Baily's Place, providing additional seating. Interestingly, in December 2004, rare books, including a copy of Audubon's masterpiece, were targeted in a failed heist at Transylvania University's library in Lexington, Kentucky. The dramatic events are retold in *American Animals*, a film blending cinematic narrative with documentary elements, starring compelling performances by Evan Peters, Barry Keoghan, Blake Jenner and Jared Abrahamson.

A man with shoulder-length curly chocolate-brown locks wearing a white stock shirt, a waistcoat and tailored trousers and carrying a sketchbook under his arm is believed to be the one and only, Mr. Audubon. His ghost is reportedly seen at dawn, peering out the windows of the Audubon Room or striding down Dauphine Street, directly in front of the hotel, as if on a mission. He vanishes without a trace as daylight unfolds.

The sign outside the Dauphine Orleans Hotel. *Courtesy of Jacob Walker, New Orleans Portrait Photography.*

Other prominent figures like Samuel Hermann Sr., a wealthy Jewish banker and commodities broker from Germany who amassed his fortune in the cotton industry, owned property on these grounds at one time. Hermann's former home, now the Hermann-Grima House Museum on St. Louis Street, stands separate from the Dauphine Orleans Hotel. However, the hotel overlooks the carriage house on the museum's property. It was originally built in the early 1830s and was later converted into the Hermann House Guest Rooms.

John James Audubon. *White House, public domain, via Wikimedia Commons.*

Guests who have stayed in these rooms are believed to have witnessed some of the sixty enslaved individuals who worked on Hermann's estate from 1831 to 1865. Reports mention sightings of dark silhouettes in ragged, threadbare clothing, moving methodically through the structure as if still tending to their appointed tasks. Guests also recount being awakened by the smell of woodsmoke and the disturbing lamentations of someone moaning and groaning as though enduring relentless labor.

In later years, significant changes reshaped the property's landscape. In the 1920s, the Hartwell Company demolished most of the original buildings on the property, marking a new phase of development by erecting a generic commercial structure on-site, which was later replaced. Construction commenced in 1967 of a multistory hotel building, initially intended to be the Bourbon Orleans Hotel. This project evolved into the luxurious Dauphine Orleans Motor Hotel and ultimately transformed into the Dauphine Orleans Hotel of today.

One of the most infamous and paranormally active structures still standing on the site is a Creole cottage that currently houses May Baily's Place, preserving the name of the renowned bordello that operated out of the structure in the late 1850s.

The story goes that May Baily immigrated to the United States from Ireland from a young age with her parents and baby sister, Millie. Her new life in New Orleans was intended to be a fresh start. She became a United States citizen and was raised in a traditional household with a doting mother and hardworking father who steadily climbed the social ranks in the city as an eminent artisan. School was something May really enjoyed, and she took pride in her studies, dreaming of one day making her mark on the world. However, when she was just a teen, her life took an unexpected turn: yellow fever claimed the lives of both her parents, leaving May and Millie destitute. Struggling to conceive of a way to financially support herself and her younger sister, May recalled stories of the seemingly glamorous and lucrative life of a madam, seeing this as the only practical solution to her glaring problem. Despite Millie's vehement opposition, May approached a wealthy friend of her late father's for assistance and, with his backing, established her own sporting house on Dauphine Street in the late 1850s, operating out of a building that had long been home to a rotating cast of families. Trying to help other young women in need who had fallen on hard times, May sought out employees for her establishment, with hopes of finding the most gorgeous women the city had to offer.

Outside May Baily's Place, a solitary red light subtly signaled to forlorn men in search of solace from women. Inside, the brothel reeked of unimaginable Victorian elegance intertwined with dark, sensual undertones. Red velvet drapes, mahogany furniture with intricate carvings, softly glowing lamps and scarlet carpeting with floral motifs oozed of period splendor. Exquisite wines and delectable cuisine were offered to men on entry, and striking beauties charmed and captivated them, ensuring their complete satisfaction.

Although May's bordello was quite high-end for what it was, at the end of the day, she was operating it illegally, and she was tired of being hit with fine after fine for running her unlawful operation. High-ranking officials, soldiers, merchants and sailors all regularly frequented her establishment and obviously loved it, spending exorbitant amounts for an evening of female companionship, so May didn't understand the pushback from the police force. Finally fed up with paying her fines piecemeal, May saved up a great deal of the cash that was flowing through the doors and eventually took the lump sum to the police station, where she paid her fines half a year in advance. Stunned by her resourcefulness and audacious behavior, the police, in turn, granted her a city license, which went into effect on May 30, 1857, under the "Ordinance Concerning Lewd and Abandoned Women," a notable law designed to control and regulate prostitution within the city limits. May's license legalized the goings-on at the establishment, and business could continue as usual, so long as certain rules were followed. It was at this time that May hired Millie, who was an adolescent, to work at the brothel. Millie begrudgingly accepted, serving her time there strictly as a barmaid.

The sign outside May Baily's Place. *Courtesy of Jacob Walker, New Orleans Portrait Photography.*

In 1861, Millie found herself drawn to a young, handsome, dark-haired, high-ranking Confederate general named Eldridge, who came into the establishment solely to play cards. Night after night, she saw him and was impressed by his willpower in avoiding sexual temptations and his profound respect of women. Before Millie knew it, she found herself falling madly in love with him, fantasizing about running off with him, leaving behind her involvement in the deviant industry her sister thrust her into. It was very apparent that Eldridge had begun feeling the same for Millie, because he started bringing his fiddle to the bordello so he could perform especially for her.

Over time, through continuous laughter, playful banter and burgeoning passion, Eldridge realized that Millie was the love of his life, and he asked to court her. Then one day, he suddenly dropped to one knee and promised her his undying love as he asked for her hand in marriage. She gleefully accepted, and together, the two lovebirds set a date for their nuptials.

This wedding meant a great deal to Millie, and May understood that. She spared no expense in the preparations for her sister, ensuring every detail was perfect. May even helped Millie acquire a breathtaking lace wedding gown, which Millie meticulously perfected for her special day. When the day arrived, Millie walked toward the altar in her sumptuous gown, filled with joy and enthusiastic expectation. However, her heart sank when Eldridge's comrades arrived with solemn expressions—without him. Confusion clouded her expression as she looked at the men, silently asking, *Where's my groom?*

What Millie did not know was that between the night before and early that morning, Eldridge's comrades had invited him out for the last time as an unmarried man. The men expected a bit of harmless fun, having a few drinks and gambling, but when Eldridge won a bag containing an unusually large amount of money in a poker game, things turned violent. The man who was on the losing end began screaming obscenities and throwing around accusations that Eldridge didn't win the money by playing fairly. Eldridge tried to defuse the situation, but before he knew it, he was staring into the barrel of a loaded gun. In a thunderous rage, the man unleashed a fatal shot, striking the general in the head. Eldridge collapsed, lifeless, on the ground.

When Millie learned of her fiancé's fate, she went into a state of hysterics. As tears streamed down her face, she rushed back to the bordello, where she began to frantically wipe down the countertops and tables as her hands trembled from her spiked adrenaline. For months, Millie neglected her own self-care, refusing to take off her wedding dress, and scrubbed every last inch of the brothel, trying to distract herself from her insurmountable grief. After a while, Millie's disregard for herself became far too noticeable to ignore. Her body emitted an odor of stale sweat that overpowered the room, her eyes were darkened by heavy bags beneath them, her nails were filled with grime and dirt from continuous cleaning, her hair was greasy and unkempt and her once impressive gown was now a tattered, filthy mess. May and the working girls decided to address the issue by forcefully holding Millie down and removing her dress so they could clean it and bathe her, but Millie flailed and thrashed her body, fighting back every step of the way. After almost a year of this ongoing battle, Millie died of a broken heart, and May was left alone in the world.

Nightly, after her death, patrons of the bordello saw Millie's ghost cleaning tables in her treasured wedding gown. To this very day, starting at sunset, her spectral figure continues to tirelessly wipe down the surfaces. Her ghost is often referred to as the White Lady, the Phantom Bride and the Lost Bride. Millie is mostly seen around the hotel bar but has been known to walk the courtyard, look out over the property from the balconies and stand near the entrance to the bar, searching and waiting for her long-lost love to return.

Anita Gomez, an entrepreneur from Los Angeles, California, briefly stayed on the property in 2016 for a business trip and recalled seeing Millie's ghost standing poolside one evening. A worried expression was etched across the bride's face as her eyes scanned the property as though she was lost in time. Thinking it was just a bride who may have had too much to drink at her reception, Anita said, "Hey girl, I'm sorry to bother you, but I just wanted to say cool dress and congratulations!" Millie looked at Anita, astounded, before burying her head in her hands and falling to her knees, letting out the most heart-wrenching and guttural wail Anita had ever heard. Millie's white form then contorted down into a ball as though she were melting into disappearance.

The encounter scared Anita so badly that she hasn't been the same since.

> *It was the craziest thing I've ever seen in my life. She looked a little rough, but she also looked very real. I mean, we were in the French Quarter; I thought she had just partied all night after her wedding and was feeling her alcohol. I thought my words would cheer her up, but it had the opposite effect. You best believe I didn't sleep a wink that night or any other night after that. How could I? I had never in my entire life seen something like that—it was like I was watching the Wicked Witch from* The Wizard of Oz *get water thrown on her in real life. Honestly, before staying at the Dauphine Orleans, I didn't even believe much in ghosts. I am most definitely a believer now!*

While Millie's ghost mourns her departed love, the ghost of a perturbed Confederate general has also been seen in the courtyard and heard pacing back and forth outside of guests' rooms. One night, a guest was jolted from sleep to find him drifting through Room 420. Do you believe this to be the spirit of Eldridge?

There is no way to say for sure, but if it is him, what a beautiful happily ever after it would be for Millie and Eldridge to cross paths on the other side, especially since they often like to share space in the courtyard. Unfortunately, many guests despise the general's obnoxious stomping, waking people from a dead sleep and being heard all night long. One such incident was documented on the comedic paranormal investigative YouTube show *Buzzfeed Unsolved*, when cast members Ryan Bergara and Shane Madej stayed in Room 101, one of the carriage rooms. According to hotel staff, the carriage rooms once served as the extended rear wing of May Baily's Place and were where May and Millie actually lived during the days of the bordello being in operation. Throughout the night, Ryan was kept awake by the sound of footsteps on the balcony above their room. When he went out to investigate the noise, nothing could be seen. Only two rooms are above Room 101, and only one of them was occupied at the time. When Ryan interviewed the guests staying in the room above, he found out that they had been there for several days and had the exact same experience, feeling fearful after being kept awake all night by the sound of loudly clomping boots outside their room.

The spectral encounters extend beyond Millie and Eldridge. Other mysterious apparitions and lingering spirits have been reported; some even say May Baily's spirit is anchored to the bar.

In the years leading up to 1915, as Storyville approached its demise, May's business appeared to decline as she turned to the streets for survival, using the alias Broadwey Rose. The New Orleans Police Department's arrest records from 1881 to 1931 reveal she lived a transient lifestyle, moving frequently and periodically becoming homeless. The sex industry had hardened May, making her tough and cunning. She often stood in doorways soliciting sex, despite this being illegal, and faced frequent arrests for it, as well as for disturbing the peace, reviling the police, lying in the streets and public drunkenness. She also accosted men and habitually lied, perhaps even repeatedly deceiving the police about her age, presenting herself as much younger than she really was. Police documents list her birth year as ranging from 1879 to 1888—a detail that doesn't align with the long-standing claim that she received her brothel license in 1857. It's challenging to accept any of her recorded birth years as accurate due to these inconsistencies, especially given her varying age (according to arrest records), which fluctuated by as much as ten years within the same year. Based on my research, I am inclined to believe she was much older than she let on. May had a reputation as a master manipulator who navigated a rough and violent existence, doing whatever it took to survive, even at the cost of harming others. Her chaotic and tumultuous later years were defined by these struggles.

On any given day, staff at May Baily's Place experience glasses being hurled from the bar, inexplicable humanlike sounds, such as pleasurable moaning and heavy grunting, and conversations heard from the Bordello Suite (111) above the bar while it is empty—a place where both sex workers

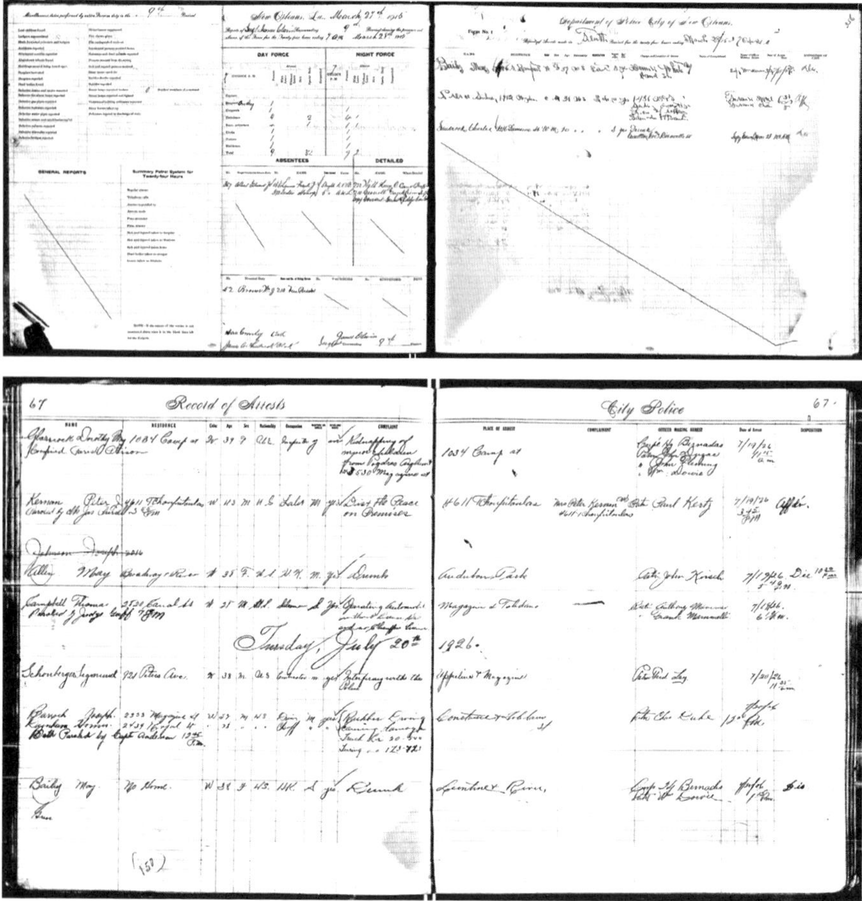
Record of Arrests

City Police

Tuesday, July 20th

1926.

Top: One of many arrest records from the New Orleans Police Department featuring May Baily, dated March 28, 1915. *Courtesy of Ancestry.com.*

Bottom: Another arrest record from the New Orleans Police Department referencing May Baily (her name is misspelled), dated July 20, 1926. *Courtesy of Ancestry.com.*

and paying customers are rumored to have been killed. Male visitors have been heard calling out for help from the bar's bathroom after being locked inside with no way out. Could this be May unleashing her pent-up aggression after the world turned her out? Some seem to think so. But there are many other ladies of the night still bound to the old bordello who don't have any plans to vacate anytime soon.

Scantily clad women are a common sight at the bar, and sometimes it's difficult to determine who is real and who is a figment of the past. The Courtesan, as she's known, is the most prevalent lady of the night at May

Baily's Place and has been known to reorganize bottles of booze, much to the dismay of the bartenders on staff. She has also been known to tamper with drinks, making men's drinks unusually strong and bitter. She's also a bit forward—more than one gentleman has felt the ghostly sensation of fingers teasing his inner thighs as he sits alone at the bar, as if she's still working the room, looking for her next rendezvous. If you choose to stay in the hotel's spookiest suites, 110 and 111, know that they come with the guarantee of a restless night. Guest testimonials describe beds that seem to bounce up and down on their own and the sounds of squeaking springs filling the silence, as if two invisible people are roughly doing the deed. Haunting wails can be heard, and glowing neon eyes have been known to peer out from the closets opposite the beds, closely watching those who dare to sleep in these rooms. It is said that Suite 110 has a more menacing spirit who prevents guests from entering the room, even when they've just unlocked the door. Covers and sheets are abruptly ripped off people's bodies, and curtains are whipped open forcefully. Housekeepers often have the power cut off on them while tending to this room and occasionally find themselves locked in. Suite 111 has a male spirit named George that tends to look out for the safety of the guests and bolts the door shut for them if they forget to lock it.

Another guest staying in an undisclosed room on the property became highly uncomfortable when she unlocked her room to find a peculiar elderly man standing inside. The man confirmed with the guest that everything was alright with her, and after being assured that it was, she kindly asked him to leave her room and promptly showed him the door. The older man complied, exited the room, headed down the hallway and disappeared.

On a property full of troubled ghosts, there exists a rare lighthearted presence: a young girl known simply as Jewel. Jewel, somewhere between ages twelve and fifteen, just so happens to be the courtyard's most joyous and popular spirit. Her peppy vibe washes over people, leaving them feeling wrapped in a bubble of comfort and warmth. She can be seen dancing alongside the hotel's quaint swimming pool with her ethereal cat at her side, who manifests as an effulgent orb. Unlike the more somber entities occupying the courtyard, Jewel is the only one that doesn't inspire sadness or fear. While she's been spotted at other French Quarter properties, spreading happiness wherever she goes, she prefers to dance at the Dauphine Orleans Hotel. Her delightful presence has also been known to help newcomers and drunken guests to their rooms at the hotel, dancing in midair the entire way. Some speculate that she worked for May Baily at one time, but Jewel exudes an innocence that seems to suggest she did not.

In essence, the Dauphine Orleans Hotel encapsulates over two centuries of history, mystery and legend. It simultaneously fascinates and terrorizes those who work and stay within its many walls, always keeping things exciting. For those eager to encounter a ghost firsthand, this historic property promises an encounter with an entire legion of the departed.

CHAPTER 4
CAPTURED IN THE DARK

ANDREW JACKSON HOTEL
919 ROYAL STREET
NEW ORLEANS, LOUISIANA 70116

Imagine for a moment that you are newly married and deeply in love. You and your partner decide to go honeymooning in New Orleans. You feel simply on top of the world. It's a few days into your trip, and you both just had the most exhilarating time out on Bourbon Street for the very first time ever. You are tipsy off Hand Grenades and Hurricanes, donning beads that locals were kind enough to throw you and slowly making your way back to your hotel through a sea of inebriated tourists and locals rushing home as lively jazz music resounds throughout the Quarter. Clutched in your hands is a disposable camera containing precious photographs that you and your partner took during your first trip to this unforgettable city. When you both finally retire to your hotel room and begin getting ready for bed, you notice your camera, sitting on the nightstand, has one shot left on it. *No problem*, you think. *We'll save the last photo for something cool we'll see tomorrow.* You both crawl into your cozy bed and quickly fall asleep, dreaming of all the places in the Big Easy you haven't had the opportunity to explore yet.

When you wake up in the morning, you go through your morning routines and decide to go out sightseeing. You're taking in the phenomenal architecture when your partner suggests a photo together. You pass your disposable camera to a stranger and ask them politely to take the last photo, but they tell you the camera isn't working. Puzzled, you take the camera back and realize the last photo no longer seems to be available. Blowing it off because you were drunk last night and maybe you misread the number of shots left, you let your partner use their camera. No big deal, right?

That evening, you take a ghost tour and are surprised to be taken by the very hotel you're staying at. The tour guide goes on and on about all the eerie happenings there, and you begin thinking it all sounds a bit too ridiculous to be true. "We're currently staying here, and we've had no personal experiences with anything remotely paranormal," you quip. The tour guide acknowledges you but assures you that your hotel is indeed one of the most haunted in the city. *It's just nonsense. These people have to make a buck somehow*, you think to yourself as the tour moves on to its next location. The rest of your stay is a blast, and you eagerly anticipate your next trip to the city.

A few days after your vacation ends, you and your partner have settled back into your regular routines, and you decide to take your camera in to get the film developed. When you go back to pick up the photographs, you're delighted to see so many amazing memories captured on film and can't wait to take them home to share with your partner. But when you get to the last picture, your heart skips a beat and your jaw drops open in horror as you realize you're looking at a shot of you and your beloved sleeping peacefully from an overhead angle, as if it was taken from the ceiling.

Sounds like the premise of a scary movie, right? The story becomes straight up bone-chilling when you consider that this exact same scenario really happened to two unfortunate souls (or fortunate, depending on your persuasion) who stayed at the Andrew Jackson Hotel in 1995. This chilling encounter is just one of many at the hotel, long rumored to be teeming with ghostly inhabitants. Perhaps this collection of spirits is due to dramatic and tragic events that unfolded in the vicinity—or even on the property itself.

During Spanish rule, the hotel grounds were home to a boys' public school that was erected in 1792 by the Spanish colonial government. The story goes that when the Great New Orleans Fire of 1794 began rapidly spreading across the city, the structure caught fire, trapping five young souls inside, where they were burned alive. The majority of the reported paranormal sightings on the property are of children's spirits, so it's understandable that so many accept this story at face value. However, newspapers and archival documents present conflicting narratives regarding the events at 919 Royal Street. One antiquated article claims the property survived the Great Fire and disputes reports of its destruction. However, the same article mentions the tragic death of five boys in a fire, adding to the uncertainty. These divergent reports underscore the challenges of historical interpretation, leaving the true fate of the property unclear.

In the late eighteenth century, New Orleans endured significant hardships, marked by three catastrophic fires that devastated the city and claimed many lives. The fire of 1778 alone destroyed 900 homes, followed by the Good Friday Fire of 1788, which consumed nearly everything in its path, leaving 856 buildings scorched. The Great New Orleans Fire of 1794, though less destructive, still resulted in the loss of 212 buildings and additional casualties. Could these calamities explain the presence of ethereal youths reportedly roaming the Andrew Jackson Hotel, even though the building itself did not burn? Absolutely! Furthermore, before the onset of yellow fever outbreaks, other diseases likely played a significant role in the high mortality rates of that era. Life expectancy averaged only thirty to forty years due to widespread diseases, harsh living conditions and inadequate medical care, so that could explain the influx of younger spirits at the property.

Another indisputable fact is that shortly after the Louisiana Purchase in 1803, the structure on the plot was converted into a United States courthouse, which came to be known as the Old Federal Courthouse. It served as the venue for federal judicial proceedings and was in operation from 1812 to 1823. Although the old courthouse was torn down in 1888, its historical significance remains. It was here that Major General Andrew Jackson, who later became the seventh president of the United States in 1829, faced legal challenges after defeating the British at the Battle of New Orleans on January 8, 1815.

Jackson's legal issues began when he overstepped his bounds and illegally declared martial law across the city of New Orleans on December 16, 1814, after becoming wary of a counterattack by British troops. With tensions running high, anyone entering or exiting the city was lawfully required to inform Jackson as a safety precaution. After learning of a naval skirmish ensuing just south of the city on January 19, 1815, Jackson feared another offensive as the British fleet grew closer to New Orleans. Although no further land invasions would take place, tensions and controversy began escalating from within the city itself.

A state legislator by the name of Louis Louaillier was displeased by General Jackson's imposition of military governance and began writing his opinions about it in a local paper. Never believing that his identity would be discovered, Louaillier publicly and boldly critiqued Jackson's authority. When Jackson read what Louaillier had written about him, his blood began to boil, and he promptly got to work on figuring out who was behind the harsh criticism. On uncovering Louallier's identity, Jackson demanded that he be arrested at once. When Judge Dominick Hall heard what happened, he took immediate action in reversing the order imposed on Louaillier, believing his detainment was unjust. He granted Louaillier a writ of habeas

Artwork depicting the Battle of New Orleans, January 8, 1815. General Andrew Jackson (on horseback, in foreground), commands American troops against British forces led by General Pakenham. Art print by Kurz and Allison, 1890. *Courtesy of Library of Congress Prints and Photographs Division.*

corpus, freeing him from imprisonment. Jackson's anger escalated into rage: he perceived the judge's actions as disregarding the safety of New Orleans. In retaliation, he ordered Judge Hall to be thrown behind bars as well, alongside Louaillier. While Jackson believed Hall's actions were a threat to his authority and the people of New Orleans, Jackson's actions were viewed as undermining Hall's jurisdiction and independence as a magistrate. Jackson eventually went as far as banishing Judge Hall from New Orleans proper until the Treaty of Ghent reached ratification status and the British departed the southern shoreline. Once the British were no longer a threat to New Orleans, Jackson revoked his order of martial law and released all prisoners, including Louaillier and Judge Hall. But when Hall returned to the city, there would be hell to pay.

After returning to New Orleans in the spring of 1815, Judge Hall summoned Jackson to appear at the courthouse. Dressed as a civilian and not someone of military prestige, Jackson appeared browbeaten before the judge as he awaited punishment. Hall made the executive decision to be the sole presider over the case and refused Jackson a trial by jury. Jackson was indicted by Hall, who held him in contempt of court and charged him with obstruction of justice, issuing him a $1,000 fine for his lengthy enactment of martial law. Locals raised money to help Jackson pay off the fine, but he refused to accept their generous donations, instead requesting that the funds be given to widows and orphans affected by the Battle of New Orleans. Congress eventually recognized Jackson for his service in keeping New Orleans safe from invasion and, in 1844, granted him funds equal to the amount of the fine, plus interest.

Andrew Jackson took his final breath on June 8, 1845, following an ongoing battle with congestive heart failure. In 1890, approximately forty-five years after Jackson's death and not long after demolition of the courthouse, a two-story building, now serving as the Andrew Jackson Hotel, was erected on the property.

For as long as the building has been used as a hotel, eerie stories from staff and guests circulated. It is said that the second floor, especially Room 208, is the most haunted area of the property. Room 208 is supposedly so haunted, in fact, that plenty of guests have struggled to last even one hour in the room after check-in.

I had the privilege of staying in Room 208 from September 30 to October 3, 2024, with my girlfriend at the time, now fiancée, Alishia Stagray. On the night of October 1, we decided to investigate the room and conducted a series of spirit box sessions, hoping to connect with any spirits that remained at the hotel. As we engaged with the device, we heard various sounds, though they had a robotic quality. Amid the static, a disembodied whisper emerged from the room, chillingly stating, "Just so you know, everything is dead." It felt as if this message was coming from right between us, as though someone were lying on the bed alongside us, dismissing our attempts to communicate.

Room 208 is reportedly the most haunted room at the Andrew Jackson Hotel. *Courtesy of Amy Shabluk.*

Despite our overall stay being enjoyable—with friendly and accommodating staff, efficient housekeepers and a cute orange resident cat named Andrew—an overwhelming discomfort washed over me during the session. Regardless of this unsettling sensation of not feeling welcomed by whatever entity resided in our room, I would 100 percent go back to the Andrew Jackson Hotel and stay again.

The otherworldly entity that occupies this room is understood to be a malignant presence masquerading as a young boy named Armand. Many believe that he died in some tragic way on the property; speculation surrounding the cause of his death ranges from suicide to homicide. We may never uncover how Armand met his end, but we know without a shadow of a doubt that he is on the property, keeping people on their toes.

Armand has been known to be very playful at times: giggling loudly, turning on water faucets, relocating guests' items to different parts of the hotel and even reaching out to tickle people during the night when they least expect it. Feeling Armand's cold finger trace their exposed arm or leg after dark leaves many disquieted. Yet Armand's demeanor can become very aggressive when one least expects it. Guests have recounted being pushed out of bed, covers being flung off them during the night, enduring extreme cold spots, being scratched until they bled by something they couldn't see and even being subjected to psychological tribulation, leaving them in a state of profound fear. These unnerving encounters are not just reserved for guests, either.

Author Nicole Beauchamp standing in front of the haunted Andrew Jackson Hotel. *Courtesy of Amy Shabluk.*

One unsettling incident unfolded when a housekeeper, after completing her tasks in the bathroom, moved on to make the bed. As she carefully tucked in a sheet, the tranquility was interrupted by a noise resembling glass shattering. She rushed back to the bathroom to investigate, finding everything undisturbed. Just as she turned to leave, a wicked, gravelly voice snarled in her ear, "*Te mataré*."

The foreboding voice spoke in Spanish, her native tongue, sending a shiver down her spine and freezing her with fear. The entity had threatened to kill her. In a frenzy, she fled from the room, only later feeling a burning sensation like that of a cat scratch and realizing claw marks marred her chest. Reluctant to reenter the room in subsequent days but committed to her work, she returned with a rosary in her pocket, only to glimpse dirty footprints sprawled across the ceiling. Soon, other housekeepers began encountering these footprints on the ceiling, too, validating her experience. Was Armand the one leaving the footprints behind? And if so, do you think he was the one who photographed the sleeping couple? While Armand's malevolent ghost predominates among the ethereal children, guests often discover Room 208 isn't the only haunted room in the building, and Armand isn't the sole presence on the second floor.

Guests entering the lobby or staying on the second floor often encounter a caretaker spirit, believed to be that of a former housekeeper. She appears as a kind-faced, petite woman of mature age, often seen tidying up the property by gently plumping pillows, adjusting towel placements and artfully rearranging furniture, luggage and even guests' shoes. At times, her presence is sensed without a physical form: guests awaken to find their shoes floating in midair or neatly arranged by the doorway. Her behavior, though occasionally unsettling, is minor compared to other reported experiences.

One morning, a guest was awakened by a rustling sensation at her feet. Opening her eyes, she was startled to see three young Spanish boys seated at the end of her bed, staring at her, which prompted her to let out a piercing scream. The boys' eyes bulged out of their pallid faces with astonishment at the jarring cry, and they screamed back before dematerializing. Terrified, the guest bolted from her room, refusing to stay another night.

In another room, a different guest woke to the sound of static from the TV, even though he had turned it off. As he reached for the remote, he froze. A ghostly boy sat on the floor, mesmerized by the screen. The man emitted a raspy shriek, and the apparition vanished instantly.

While these guests were terrified, enthusiasts of the paranormal desire such encounters, hoping for thrilling experiences that will be remembered for a lifetime. Mark Ristine from Gilbert, Pennsylvania, is a recurring visitor to the city and arranged a stay with his adult son at the hotel in May 2022. The men were eager to stay in a purportedly haunted locale, and on arrival, they were assigned a balcony room on the second floor. While they never saw the ghostly trio or any other physical apparitions during their stay, Mark and his son encountered one of the most frequently reported phenomena in

A full-length portrait of Andrew Jackson painted by D.M. Carter and engraved by A.H. Ritchie, circa 1860. *Courtesy of Library of Congress Prints and Photographs Division.*

the hotel: the persistent pitter-patter of children's footsteps in the hallways, stairwell and guest rooms.

Many guests report hearing phantom footsteps—even when they're still inside their rooms. In the case of Mark and his son, footsteps could be heard outside their door. Initially soft, the sound of the footsteps did not disturb the men, but as they persisted, they began to quicken. Sometimes it even sounded as if there were multiple sets of feet chasing each other. It sounded exactly as if children were playing.

Mark and his son investigated the noises. It appeared they were coming from both the staircase and the hallway outside their room. Mark's son tried to re-create the footsteps to determine if they could possibly be explained by another guest or maybe just a staff member walking by. However, during the re-creation, all that could be heard was the groaning of the floorboards under his son's weight and the same sound resonating from the stairwell. The phantom footsteps that had been heard over their weeklong stay didn't seem to cause the floorboards to creak at all, suggesting perhaps they were not footsteps of the living. After all, the child spirits on-site have been known to run amok all over the building and property, including rooms on both floors of the hotel, as well as the courtyard. No guest who stays at the Andrew Jackson Hotel is free from the watchful eyes of a child. Amid these strange encounters, the controversial ghost of Andrew Jackson himself is said to walk the property.

While some insist that Andrew Jackson couldn't haunt the hotel simply because it bears his name, others believe his ghost seeks retribution against Judge Hall. These skeptics may overlook that the grounds were once a courthouse where Jackson felt unjustly persecuted. Observers describe a tall, slender man in a high-collared woolen suit with tousled gray hair and piercing, icy blue eyes seen roaming the property. He startles staff by appearing when they're alone and surprises guests in their rooms before absconding into the ether.

As the tales of phantasmic encounters at the Andrew Jackson Hotel continue to captivate and disturb visitors, these accounts serve as a reminder of New Orleans' complex and poignant history, where the boundaries between past and present, reality and the supernatural, fade into obscurity. An overnight stay here may bring more than memories. Will you be the next guest to find your photo taken in the dead of night?

CHAPTER 5

IN BED WITH THE DEAD

OLIVIER HOUSE HOTEL
828 TOULOUSE STREET
NEW ORLEANS, LOUISIANA 70112

Nestled between Bourbon and Dauphine Streets stands the charming and uncanny Olivier House Hotel, featuring several historic buildings that shape its present-day structure. Among these, a three-story brick and stucco addition designed by architect Henry Grimball in 1965 stands as a noteworthy feature complementing the main historic mansion. Step inside, and you will be instantly transported to a domain where the past and present blend seamlessly. The mansion, originally constructed in 1839 for Madame Marie Anne Bienvenu Olivier ("Marie Anne" on her grave, "Marianne" according to the home's chain of title), exudes the elegant Creole and Greek Revival styles. It was designed by well-known brother architects of the era J.N.B. De Pouilly and J.I. De Pouilly. The house has endured fires and the ravages of the Civil War and even survived plans for demolition to make way for a parking lot. But amid these trials, the Olivier House Hotel stands today as a bastion of timeless allure and mystic ambiance.

Times were tough in late eighteenth-century New Orleans, and Marie Anne Bienvenu, a blossoming young woman of only sixteen who desired to maintain her comfortable lifestyle, wed Nicholas Goderoy Olivier, a Revolutionary War veteran and respected figure in the city, who was fifteen years her senior. His grandfather, dispatched by King Louis XIV of France, was instrumental in establishing the first network of roads and bridges in the Louisiana colony, which added to the family's honored eminence. Marie Anne was captivated by Nicholas's charisma and his prominent reputation. She saw in him a man who could offer the financial security and elevated social standing she had grown accustomed to growing up with her wealthy politician and plantation-owning father. Her decision to marry Nicholas was deliberate, rooted in her desire to obtain legal rights and educational opportunities and to navigate the expectations of her family and society. After the marriage, it didn't take long for the Olivier family to become one of the richest in all New Orleans.

Marie Anne and Nicholas ended up having a number of children, and after Nicholas's passing on July 18, 1815, Marie Anne received a substantial sum of money, enabling her to care for their children as well as herself. Two decades later, Marie Anne used her hefty funds to commission the building of a massive home. The newly completed residence, which came at the significant cost of $24,000, featured a secluded courtyard enclosed by a carriageway near Dauphine Street. The courtyard's original paving stones, which are present on the estate, arrived as ballast on sailing ships that returned to Europe laden with grain. Due to the extra weight of the grain, these stones were no longer needed, and they were sold off for other purposes.

Adjacent to the courtyard is a separate building containing the original kitchen, now Room 105, which still showcases the large hearth used for family meals. Farther back on the property, a livery accommodated the family's horses and carriage. The rooftop, along with the interior of the stately home, were built with wooden beams that came from flatboats that floated down the Mississippi River in the early 1800s carrying goods such as flour, grain and livestock. These boats were dismantled for timber, and the wood was repurposed for construction. Square notches or round holes in the beams can still be seen today and indicate where pegs or mortises were once employed. Inside the main structure, visitors were greeted by a spacious entry hall, a formal dining area and an expansive double parlor on the ground floor, largely retaining the layout from Madame Olivier's era.

Upstairs, the main house boasted a second-story master bedroom and a grand ballroom, complemented by additional bedrooms accessible via a winding staircase. Originally intended as slave quarters, the upper-floor rooms surrounding the courtyard were accessed via a stairwell hidden within an arched alcove, which is now out of use. Contemporary accounts lauded the interiors for their refined elegance and superior craftsmanship.

Madame Olivier's time in the magnificent residence was brief, as she passed away on February 2, 1843. However, she left a lasting legacy. She was a pivotal figure in New Orleans Creole society, wielding considerable influence in shaping the city's social and cultural fabric. At the time of her

828 Toulouse Street as it appeared in 1938. *Courtesy of Carnegie Survey of the Architecture of the South, Library of Congress, Prints and Photographs Division.*

death, she was beloved as a mother, grandmother and great-grandmother to over sixty descendants. On Madame Olivier's passing, the property passed through several hands before it entered a new chapter as a summer home under the ownership of George Raymond Locoul, who went by Raymond, and his wife, Elisabeth, née Duparc.

Raymond was a native of France who immigrated to New Orleans and owned vineyards throughout Bordeaux. This served Elisabeth well in the long run, as her husband had ownership of the property for only a little over a month before he passed away from yellow fever. Elisabeth began selling off wine from the vineyards, importing over ten thousand bottles into the United States, which she stored at her ancestral estate in Vacherie, a sugar plantation that was originally called L'habitation Duparc (the Duparc Dwelling), is now known as the Laura Plantation (named after Elisabeth's granddaughter Laura Locoul Gore) and is currently open to the public for tours. When Elisabeth's father, Guillaume Duparc, died in 1808, her mother, Nanette Prud'homme, assumed responsibility for the daily operations of the farm, marking the beginning of four generations of women who would oversee the plantation.

Nanette retired in 1829 and formally transferred control of the sugar plantation to her three children, Louis, Flagy and Elisabeth, on August 7 that same year through the incorporation of the family business, Duparc Frères et Locoul. This arrangement persisted until April 8, 1856. It was then that Elisabeth, who survived both her parents and her elder brothers, assumed leadership of the plantation. She oversaw the farm during the entirety of the Civil War and most of the Reconstruction period that followed it.

During the Civil War, Union soldiers commandeered the Olivier House for military operations, subjecting it to severe damage and neglect. Despite their destructive actions, they notably spared the upper floors where family members slept, likely due to the presence of a trunk displaying Masonic symbols belonging to Raymond. This gesture was thought to reflect a perceived respect among Freemasons in the Northern army toward symbols of Freemasonry in the Southern states, sparing the house from further harm during this tumultuous period. After the war, Elisabeth, in her resilience, revived the home to its past magnificence. The throes of war made Elisabeth, who was always a devout Catholic, even more serious about her religion, and she prayed over her home daily, thankful to have it back in her hands once again.

By the 1870s, Elisabeth was living in the Olivier House full time, and in due time, she split possession of the farm equally between her son, Louis Raymond Emile, known primarily as Emile, and her daughter, Mary Elisabeth Aimée, known primarily as Aimée. Emile would go on to name the plantation after his firstborn daughter.

After Elisabeth's death inside the Olivier House on November 1, 1882, Aimée held stewardship over both the plantation and the Olivier House, while living primarily in Paris. During her time in France, she met and married Monsieur Ivan Charles de Lobel-Mahy, a French count. Following Aimée's stewardship, her daughter Françoise inherited the mansion. Françoise, entering the realms of prominence, married Monsieur Paul D'Abzac, a distinguished French viscount, diplomat for the French Republic and accomplished writer. His career spanned multiple international assignments, including a post in New Orleans, during which the couple resided at the Olivier House.

When the neighboring French Opera House succumbed to flames on December 4, 1919, the city was left in devastation. For decades, this venue was a cornerstone of society until it fell victim to a fierce blaze. Remarkably, the Olivier House, which had been standing just one building away for two decades, emerged largely unscathed, leaving only charred patches on its elegant façade.

In the 1920s, Salvatore Valenti, an Italian man who possessed neighboring property, was looking for a place to operate a funeral parlor. After Françoise granted Salvatore a temporary lease, the Olivier House became a solemn venue for a multitude of wakes and funerals. The house saw a constant flow of deceased individuals passing through its doorways. Cries of mourning echoed through the structure as cold, lifeless bodies were laid out in what is currently the guests' parlor. The home became a gateway that countless souls passed through, some never departing.

In 1940, Françoise sold the home to Bessie Brown and her husband, George, before moving permanently to Paris. The Browns purchased the spacious home without ever setting foot on the property, following Bessie's inheritance and subsequent sale of her family's plantation in Mississippi. She had been uninterested in maintaining the plantation, and after George's death in 1945 (Françoise passed the same year), Bessie found the expansive New Orleans residence too large for solitary living. Seeking to utilize the space and generate income, Bessie began accommodating individuals interested in staying temporarily or long term.

As the 1950s dawned, the Olivier House faced the threat of "progress." In 1959, plans were unveiled by Centex Corporation, a housing developing company out of Dallas, Texas, to erect a hotel on the site of the former opera house, a long-used parking lot situated next to the Olivier House. Though the proposed hotel aimed to harmonize architecturally with the surrounding French Quarter, the plans meant the historic mansion would be demolished to make way for the hotel's parking garage, prompting outcry from preservationists. This echoed their earlier efforts in 1938 to save the adjacent Formento house at 826 Toulouse, the only structure that stood between the mansion and the French Opera House during the fire. While 826 Toulouse was not spared, the Olivier House was, and it underwent significant renovations in the 1960s, transforming it into modern apartments.

James "Jim" and Kathryn Danner (née Flucke) acquired the property in 1972, transitioning it into a forty-two-room boutique hotel. The daily operations at the hotel are now carried out by their descendants.

The Olivier House Hotel still welcomes guests today, and those who've stayed on the property share tales of spooky happenings that plagued them during their visit. It is strongly believed that both Madame Olivier and Madame Locoul continue to haunt the very rooms they once graced. Joining them are the spectral manifestations of a soldier and a ghostly cat and invisible humanlike presences that, late at night, are known to crawl into bed with unsuspecting guests. While the spirits tend to be a benign bunch at the Olivier House Hotel, their eerie presence unnerves many.

When the sun sets, the sweet scents of rose and jasmine begin to permeate the air of the hotel's upper levels, suffusing the corridors with a nostalgic fragrance that transports guests to another era. Footsteps echo faintly on the aged floorboards, heralding the arrival of a specter in Victorian dress and coiffed hair believed to be Madame Olivier. Her face bears a demeanor both kind and serious, a subtle smile softening her otherwise austere expression, reflecting her delicate and dignified nature. She means no bother to guests, gracefully wandering the old mansion as she did in life, the only sounds she produces a sweet humming and the gentle swishing of her elaborate dress.

As Madame Olivier's presence brings a sense of serene familiarity to the property, the ghost of Madame Locoul is thought to be more stirring to guests due to the disembodied whispers that accompany her. The purported spirit of Madame Locoul, draped in a flowing black antebellum gown and adorned with a white lace cap, clasps a rosary tightly in her hands, her fingers tracing the beads with a practiced, rhythmic motion. Sometimes, she holds them closely to her mouth as the soft murmur of continuous prayers escapes her lips. Her spirit is often seen meandering around the ground floor and traversing the stairwells in the daylight hours, her muted reciting of the Hail Mary barely audible yet hauntingly persistent as her figure intermittently manifests and dissipates.

While the ethereal presence of these matriarchs remains understated, other spirits make their presence known in more palpable ways, prompting many guests to hastily request a room change or notify the front desk of their departure, requiring staff to retrieve their belongings.

At check-in, guests are greeted by three adorable resident house cats, a charming introduction to their stay. However, as night falls, some guests feel the undeniable sensation of a cat jumping onto their bed. Initially assuming it's one of the house cats, they are perplexed when, on turning on the light, no visible cat is present. Instead, they discover a telltale indentation on the bed, as if an invisible feline is sleeping there. When they fluff the sheets to remove the indentation, the bed appears normal again. However, as the guests settle back into bed, they feel the sensation of a cat jumping up once more, and the indentation reappears. At other times, the feline appears just as visible as the other cats on-site, fading into nothingness when guests attempt to pet it. Skeptical guests search the room high and low, thinking the cat has bolted into a hiding spot. A quick call to the front desk confirms that every resident cat is already accounted for. Michelle E. wrote a review on TripAdvisor after her February 2018 stay at the hotel and specified that although she did not see a ghost, she did experience the sensation of a ghost cat jumping off her bed around five o'clock in the morning. While she didn't specify the exact room she stayed in, she did indicate it was on an upper floor. Whose mysterious cat could this be? While they remain a mystery, these occurrences are thought of as entertaining by most guests, but you know what's not? Feeling someone cuddle up against you when your partner is sleeping in front of you or you're alone.

In reviews from all across the internet, guests recount experiencing the sensation of someone getting into bed with them, sometimes even multiple times in a night. According to a comment on the *Haunted Nation* blog dated December 15, 2021, an anonymous guest reported experiencing something or someone lying next to them on three occasions in Room 405. They became aware of the haunting only midway through their three-day stay. Another anonymous guest who stayed in Room 402 wrote a comment on April 23, 2021, explaining that they didn't feel alone in their room and that they heard footsteps consistently pacing by their bedside. Other reviews were vague about their room numbers but open about the fact that they were terrified to sense someone snuggling up to them in the night—especially those who were staying alone. One guest actually felt someone wrap their arm around her waist and turned to see no one beside her.

For those seeking a brush with the dead, Rooms 104, 106, 206 and the Honeymoon Suite 216 at the Olivier House Hotel are believed to be the most active. However, in true New Orleans fashion, any room on the property offers the chance to experience something otherworldly. Two of these rooms were featured on the YouTube show *My Ghost Story* by the UnXplained Zone.

Nemo Purat had always been skeptical about ghosts. His mother, who worked as a front desk clerk at the hotel, often shared tales of spectral encounters, but Nemo dismissed them as fanciful stories, having stayed at the hotel three times without incident. His fourth stay in Room 104 would change everything.

One evening, a friend who worked in the French Quarter joined him at the hotel for a night of fun after leaving work. Laughing off the haunting rumors, they joked about summoning Elisabeth's spirit, as Room 104 was her bedroom and the place where she supposedly passed away—unaware of the chilling consequences that awaited.

Alone after his friend left for work, Nemo decided to unwind with a bath. Yet as he soaked, an uneasy feeling crept over him, accompanied by strange taps echoing through the room. Initially dismissive, he soon found it harder to ignore.

At three thirty in the morning, Nemo woke abruptly, the warmth of the room replaced by an icy chill that seized his body. Unable to move, he watched in terror as a white orb of light materialized and hovered above him. The room grew colder, his heart racing as the orb circled the bed, drawing nearer with each pass.

With a sudden burst of speed, the orb darted away, leaving Nemo shaken and fearful. Unable to stay another moment, he hurried to the night clerk, desperate to escape the room's spectral inhabitant. Sensing his distress, the clerk swiftly gathered Nemo's belongings, and he fled the hotel, vowing never to return. From that night on, Nemo Purat's skepticism of the supernatural was shattered. His encounter in Room 104 left him a believer—an experience that continues to haunt him.

Jerry Venis had grown accustomed to the quirks of Room 206, where he had stayed at least twenty times over the years. He believed he had encountered the ghost of Elisabeth on several of his stays at the property. At the close of the day, Jerry and his companion were relaxing in the room, enjoying a cigarette despite Elisabeth's rumored disapproval of smoking. As they chatted, the sounds of Bourbon Street drifted in through the balcony door, prompting them to step outside briefly to see what was happening.

On returning to the room, they were met with a puzzling sight: the ashtray they'd been using had vanished, replaced by a bottle of water sitting neatly on the coffee table. Jerry knew they hadn't brought water up with them, and there was no logical explanation for how it had appeared there. Jerry surmised it was Elisabeth's way of expressing her disdain for their smoking.

Undeterred by the odd occurrence, Jerry and his partner continued their evening, sharing stories and laughter late into the night. However, as the hours passed, subtle signs of Elisabeth's presence began to make themselves known. Before bed, Jerry struggled to secure the chain lock on the door. After several failed attempts, he finally managed to hook the chain into place, feeling a brief sense of relief. However, when morning dawned, he was bewildered to find the chain lock unsecured and hanging limply.

On another occasion, Jerry snapped a photo of his companion and, when the film was developed, was astonished to find a dozen orbs hovering in the image, a phenomenon often associated with paranormal activity. The photograph served as a tangible reminder of the unseen forces at play within the hotel's historic walls. In another photograph, Jerry managed to capture something even more concrete: a faint but unmistakable silhouette of a woman in an antebellum-style dress, her ghostly form standing on the stairwell. These encounters left Jerry Venis both intrigued and spooked about the Olivier House Hotel. For him, each visit was not just a stay in a historic mansion but also a journey into the unknown.

In addition to Elisabeth's presence, the lone spirit of a Union soldier has been seen standing in the hallway outside of Room 206, a reminder of the days when Northern forces occupied the home.

The Olivier House Hotel exemplifies the uniqueness of New Orleans, radiating character at every turn. Each visit offers an exclusive glimpse into the past, where architectural beauty and cultural heritage coexist. Staying at the Olivier House is more than just a lodging experience; it's an invitation to become part of the house's ongoing story. For those who revel in the unusual: you may just find yourself in bed with the dead.

CHAPTER 6

SHADOWS OF SUFFERING

OMNI ROYAL ORLEANS HOTEL
621 SAINT LOUIS STREET
NEW ORLEANS, LOUISIANA 70130

At the corner of Saint Louis and Royal Streets, the Omni Royal Orleans Hotel stands as a beacon of elegance. As you step into the hotel's grand marble lobby, your eyes are treated to the warm glow of glistening crystal chandeliers. With 345 meticulously appointed rooms, including three exclusive suites, the hotel offers year-round amenities such as a unique rooftop fitness center, an inviting heated outdoor pool and an observation deck providing panoramic views of the French Quarter and the Mississippi River. Guests can savor exquisite meals at the Rib Room, grab quick snacks and coffee at Morsels or unwind at La Riviera poolside bar and Touché Bar. Every stay promises unparalleled distinction embodying the pinnacle of luxury. Yet beneath this façade of grandeur lies a history of darkness, sorrow and even a few ghosts.

In the early nineteenth century, New Orleans' port attracted merchants and ships from around the globe, driven by a thriving trade in sugarcane and cotton. The intersection where the Omni Royal Orleans Hotel stands today was bustling with activity, primarily that of the Creole elite. During the antebellum period, Chartres Street was a vibrant spectacle, akin to Broadway, lined with elegant Parisian-style establishments. Saint Louis Street, which was central to the cultural and political life of the local community, further enhanced this lively atmosphere. This corner housed *L'Abeille de la Nouvelle Orléans*, the largest French-language newspaper in the area, making it a media epicenter where the local populace accessed crucial information. Within a one-block radius, nearly every major profession had a presence. Yet beneath this dynamic surface, the crossroads also harbored a darker side, serving as a focal point for human trafficking.

Long before the Omni Royal Orleans Hotel was built, the site hosted several exclusive exchanges, colloquially known as coffeehouses. These male-only establishments, intended for White businessmen, were central to high society. The term *coffeehouse* derives from the French *maison de café*, referring to a place serving coffee in the morning and alcohol in the evening. These exchanges were not just social hubs but also pivotal centers of business, recreation and networking, and they were a key factor in the trade of human lives, facilitating transactions over coffee and alcohol between those dealing in individuals held in bondage.

Tremoulet's Commercial Coffee House opened in 1810 at Chartres and Saint Louis, catering to this elite clientele. Pierre Maspero took over in 1814, renaming it Maspero's Exchange, and it later became Elkin's Exchange after Maspero's death in 1822. By 1826, John Hewlett, a Creole-born businessman of mixed French and Black heritage, had begun managing

A historic photograph from 1937–38 of the building at 440 Chartres Street, best known as Maspero's Exchange. *Courtesy of Carnegie Survey of the Architecture of the South, Library of Congress, Prints and Photographs Division.*

the establishment, renaming it Hewlett's Exchange. As his business grew, Hewlett formed a partnership with a man named Bright, founding the firm Hewlett and Bright. In May 1835, their partnership was actively involved in the slave trade, selling enslaved individuals, including families of various ages. With his growing success, Hewlett sought to expand his business even further.

Hewlett's Exchange became a testament to opulence, reflecting Hewlett's expensive taste and love of money. The two-story building, measuring fifty-five by sixty-two feet, stood proudly at 501 Chartres. Although it no longer exists, a similar historic structure can be found at the corner of 440 Chartres, where Pierre Maspero's Restaurant now resides. Entering through the elaborate Venetian screens, men encountered glossy marble and rich wooden interiors beneath soaring nineteen-foot ceilings. The room was illuminated by four stunning chandeliers and walls featuring oil paintings of a lewd sexual nature, geographical maps and portraits of American and French political figures, such as George Washington and Napoleon. A massive bar, stocked with the finest liquors and outfitted with glassware imported from France, stood as a centerpiece. The upper floors of Hewlett's Exchange offered entertainment, with billiards and gambling tables available for visitors. The heart of the building, however, was the auction hall. It was here where seven auctioneers, including Joseph Le Carpentier, Toussaint Mossy, H.J. Domingue, George Boyd, Joseph Baudue, François Dutillet and Isaac McCoy, took turns presiding over auctions six days a week.

From ten o'clock in the morning to three o'clock in the afternoon, the auctioneers conducted lively bidding in French, Spanish and English as merchants and city elites engaged in buying and selling. The contrast between grandeur and suffering was palpable. Enslaved individuals, dressed in fine clothing for the "occasion," forced themselves to smile to avoid further mistreatment while being paraded before a crowd often indifferent to their plight. Abolitionists were deeply unsettled by their forced demeanor, finding it eerily out of place but recognizing it as a desperate attempt to avoid harsher treatment. Their true distress only became apparent when they reached the auction block, where their fear and anguish were made visible—most prevalently in those with children. One heart-wrenching example was that of a mother being ripped away from her three children while the crowd ignored their pitiful sobbing. Purchasers concentrated on only the physical condition of the slaves, disregarding any consideration of their mental or emotional misery. Buyers scrupulously examined each slave's mouth and limbs, particularly the flexibility and strength of their joints. Any signs of frequent or severe flogging on their upper bodies marked them as defiant and difficult to control, making them less desirable for purchase.

When Abraham Lincoln visited New Orleans in 1828 and again in 1831, as a young man, it's entirely possible that he may have witnessed the harsh realities of Hewlett's Exchange: after all, it was *the* place to be for anybody who was somebody back in that era. In 1830 alone, 4,435 enslaved individuals were sold in the city. Given the central role of Hewlett's Exchange, it likely handled a significant portion of these transactions—potentially at least a quarter and perhaps even more than a third of the total.

As Hewlett observed the immense profits flowing through his exchange, his ambitions grew. Driven by greed and a desire for greater status, he envisioned a more opulent exchange that would outshine his current, already lavish establishment. Additionally, as an aspiring hotelier, Hewlett sought to integrate his fancy new exchange into a grand hotel that would multiply his income. He believed that such a project would attract more visitors, increase his wealth and elevate his social standing. To realize this vision, Hewlett began seeking someone who could help make this visionary and profitable venture a reality.

In 1835, amid the rivalry between the city's Creole and American sections, the Improvement Bank engaged architect J.N.B. De Pouilly to develop a prestigious hotel designed to impress the city's European community. De Pouilly and Hewlett shared the same vision and partnered up with the goal of surpassing the success of the American-run St. Charles Hotel in what is now the Central Business District (CBD). Their combined efforts resulted in the creation of the St. Louis Hotel & Exchange. The structure was designed to emulate Paris's Rue de Rivoli. However, the financial turmoil of the Panic of 1837 forced a significant reduction in scope, resulting in a more modest version of the original plan. Nonetheless, the hotel still was certainly a sight to behold. As part of this monumental undertaking, all businesses on the site had to be demolished to make way for the new landmark, which spanned an entire city block bordered by Royal, Toulouse, Chartres and Saint Louis Streets.

The St. Louis Hotel, also known as the St. Louis Exchange Hotel, was in operation by 1838. It quickly gained acclaim as one of New Orleans' most prestigious establishments, celebrated for its lavish social events and high-society gatherings. The hotel was renowned for its opulent décor and amenities, including bespoke cocktails and billiards, which captivated elite visitors. Per Hewlett, it continued to function as a center for the trading of captives, known then as the New Orleans Exchange, becoming a prominent market in the city and the Deep South.

The St. Louis Hotel's ornate rotunda became a notable venue for auctions, featuring a range of items from artworks to merchandise and, regrettably, human beings. Held beneath a grand eighty-eight-foot dome surrounded by towering Tuscan columns, these auctions stood in stark contrast to the more dismal ones held on the streets and in levees, residences and slave pens. These prisonlike structures housed fifty to one hundred people under deplorable conditions and were situated in bordering faubourgs, which are suburbs or districts located on the outskirts of the city. Although the auctions at the St. Louis Hotel were considered high-end and were promoted with extensive newspaper advertising, they represented the same inhumane exploitation.

On February 11, 1840, the original hotel was engulfed by an all-devouring blaze, completely leveling the fantastic architecture. After the fire, the hotel was rapidly reconstructed with financial support from the nearby Citizens Bank, costing $600,000. The rebuilt structure included innovative fire-resistant design elements, such as a lightweight rotunda built with hollow clay pots arranged in a honeycomb pattern. By 1842, it was back to receiving guests and continuing its grim role in the slave trade. During this period, the selling of human lives at the hotel was booming.

During auctions, enslaved individuals were forced onto a raised wooden platform called the slave block as auctioneers took turns describing their height, strength and health in multiple languages. Around them, the wealthy, attired in high fashion, indulged in gilded comforts and excesses. John Theophilus Kramer vividly describes this scene: "Richly dressed gentlemen are helping themselves to fine liquors and delicacies [while] ladies, splendidly dressed in black silk and satin, and glittering with precious jewels, are entering the hall." The display of precious stones and finery at such events offered a glimpse into the wealthy's vanity and avarice, exposing their disregard for human dignity as they flaunted their social status amid the ruthless trade of individuals.

These auctions, often linked to the liquidation of deceased wealthy slaveholders' estates or financial debts, drew significant attention. Smaller dealers occasionally contributed their captives, typically the young and robust, to these high-profile city auctions. The barbaric perception of people of color as animals rather than human beings was mirrored in sale records, which further reduced them to derogatory racial labels: negro (Black), mulatto (biracial), griffe (of African and Native American descent), quadroon (one-quarter Black) and octoroon (one-eighth Black), terms twisted by traders to manipulate prices. Families were torn apart and dehumanized as they were displayed and appraised with cold indifference. Prices were set with clinical detachment: $750 for a husband, $550 for a wife and $250 for each child. Transactions concluded with formal documentation, transferring the individual to the buyer as property, thus perpetuating their subjugation. The gritty details of these transactions were observed by spectators like George Buckingham, who happened on an auction while passing through the rotunda during its reopening in 1842 and provided personal testimony about the blatant inhumanity he witnessed.

The notoriety of the rotunda at the former St. Louis Hotel inspired Harriet Beecher Stowe's depiction of slaves being sold off at an auction in a hotel rotunda in her 1852 novel *Uncle Tom's Cabin*. Tragically, these auctions remained a fixture until the Civil War began. The war's impact caused a rapid decline in the hotel's popularity. As the building became a shell of its former self, it was repurposed to accommodate troops during this period of emptiness.

Sale of Estates, Pictures, and Slaves in the Rotunda, New Orleans, by William Henry Brooke, engraver. Hand-colored engraving (original 1842), presented here in black and white. *Courtesy of the Historic New Orleans Collection, 1974.25.23.4.*

John Hewlett wasted no time in turning his attention to the American side of town, where he established a new version of Hewlett's Exchange at the corner of Common and Camp Streets. His decision to move to this side of the city highlighted his shift from Creole to American interests, driven by a quest for greater profit. Eventually, Hewlett expanded this venture into another hotel, further cementing his alignment with American commercial interests over loyalty to his Creole heritage.

In 1884, a new hotel opened on the same site where the St. Louis Hotel once stood: the Hotel Royal. According to the *Daily Picayune*, it had "sprung into grandeur from out of the decayed and ancient hull of the old hostelry." The hotel featured four hundred rooms, a bar, three large dining rooms, parlors and a ladies' entrance on Royal Street. It sought to capitalize on the legacy of the former St. Louis Hotel, but by 1906, the once grand building had already slipped into disrepair. Tourists began exploring the derelict structure, while the homeless sought refuge within its crumbling walls.

The old slave block in the former St. Louis Hotel, circa 1906. *Courtesy of Detroit Publishing Company photograph collection (Library of Congress).*

This photograph of the old slave block at the former St. Louis Hotel features a woman who was sold there as a child; it was later turned into a postcard. *Courtesy of the Historic New Orleans Collection, gift of Alan Freedman and Patricia Mysza of the Midwest Center for Justice, Evanston, Illinois, 2015.0127.1.*

Then the Great Storm of 1915, a devastating Category 4 hurricane with winds reaching 145 miles per hour, wreaked havoc on the already deteriorating hotel. The imposing structure finally met its fate—a wrecking ball—in 1916, leaving only a few utilitarian buildings behind. Before the rotunda's destruction, the infamous slave block was thoroughly photographed and the images were turned into postcards, a bizarre and audacious choice for a keepsake. It's almost incomprehensible that people thought a memento of such suffering would make an acceptable souvenir. What were they thinking? Sadly, this pattern persists, as evidenced by postcards from places like former concentration camps, suggesting that our mindset hasn't changed as much as we'd like to believe.

The site remained vacant for decades. Then, in 1960, another hotel emerged: the Royal Orleans Hotel, developed by Edgar B. Stern with the help of Lester B. Kabacoff and the Hotel Corporation of America. Architects Samuel Wilson Jr. and Arthur Q. Davis designed a modern structure that paid homage to the St. Louis Hotel's former glory. The Royal Orleans Hotel initially did very well, but due to a multitude of factors—including rising

A glimpse of the Hotel Royal around 1906. *Courtesy of Detroit Publishing Company photograph collection (Library of Congress).*

Above: The front entrance of the Omni Royal Orleans Hotel. *Courtesy of Jacob Walker, New Orleans Portrait Photography.*

Opposite: The staircase on the right-hand side is where Henry Figueroa witnessed the spirit of a distraught female slave. *Courtesy of Amy Shabluk.*

competition, evolving market conditions and changes in consumer tastes—its appeal declined over time. In 1980, the property was sold to Aetna Life Insurance Company and then to the Sonesta Corporation and, finally, in 1986, to Omni Hotels and Resorts, under whose auspices it thrives to this day. Many say the hotel continues to host not only living guests but also the traumatized souls of those who never left.

In early December 2014, Henry Figueroa and his wife traveled to the Crescent City with their youngest daughter to celebrate her fortieth birthday. Wanting to make her milestone birthday one to remember and impress her parents, Henry's daughter chose the hotel due to its grandiose ambiance. At sundown, Henry waited in the hotel lobby people-watching while his wife and daughter finished getting ready for their dinner reservations. Out of nowhere, Henry began hearing the sound of someone softly sobbing, which at first seemed faint and distant. As time went on, the subdued weeping gradually grew more intense, eventually transforming into full-blown wailing. He initially brushed it off, as he didn't see anyone nearby, so he chose not to pay it much attention, but now he could no longer ignore it.

Henry stood up as his eyes scanned the lobby intensively, searching for the source. When he didn't see anyone on the main level, he cast his eyes downward over the banister of the staircase and saw a young woman, no older than twenty-five, in a flowered cotton dress with a starched white apron and a turbaned handkerchief, sitting at the bottom of the stairs, her

head buried in her hands. As he gripped the railing to get a better look, his wedding ring gently clanking against the metal caught the woman's attention, causing her to look up at him. The crimson hue of her bloodshot eyes and her tear-stained cheeks, indicative of despondence, unmoored him, causing him to hurriedly make his way to the front desk, where the receptionist was accommodating another guest.

Trying to wait patiently but unable to stop himself, Henry interrupted their conversation. "Excuse me, but what are you going to do about the lady who is wailing at the bottom of your staircase?"

Both the employee and the guest made eyes at one another as if to say, *What is this man on about?* The receptionist turned to Henry. "I'm sorry, sir. I don't know what you're talking about," he said, and continued helping the guest he was with.

This response irritated Henry, who could still hear the sobbing echoing loudly throughout the spacious lobby. "Good God, man! How can you not hear that? It's louder than hell!"

The receptionist, trying not to aggravate Henry further, said, "Please allow me a moment to finish up with this guest and I will be right with you, sir."

Henry responded, "I'm sorry, this needs to be addressed now. There is a young woman bawling her eyes out at the bottom of your stairs. I think she may be hurt."

Looking as if he had no other choice, the receptionist turned reluctantly to the other guest and said, "I'm sorry, ma'am. Do you mind giving me just a moment to address this?" The guest nodded as she rolled her eyes, obviously peeved at having to wait.

Henry led the receptionist to the banister, where he motioned down to the unconsolable woman. The agent cautiously stated, "Sir, I'm very sorry. I don't see anyone. Perhaps she left. I really need to help the guest I was with, but if she comes back, please let me know." He turned to walk away.

Henry erupted in anger. "Are you kidding me?! Wow, you're really professional, walking away from someone in need. Whatever, I'll check on her myself!" He proceeded down the stairwell to check on the crying woman, and with each step he took, she became fainter. When Henry got to where she'd been sitting, she was completely gone.

As he stood on the steps, stumped, his wife and daughter appeared at the top of the staircase. "There you are! We were wondering where you were! Ready to roll?"

Henry looked at them, dazed, as he collected himself. "Yep, I could use a stiff drink right about now."

Henry's encounter was not an isolated incident. Other guests who stayed at the hotel also experienced the apparitions of former slaves and heard their heartbreaking cries and pained moans all over the property. These seemingly residual spirits, however, are known to vanish before anyone can interact with them.

Another guest, who stayed on the seventh floor, reported an eerie encounter after stepping out of the bathroom following a shower. As she crossed the threshold, still damp and wrapped in only a towel, her eyes were drawn to the window, and she froze in horror at the presence of a man, shackled at the wrists and ankles, who stood staring blankly outside.

Her heart hammered in her chest like a succession of drums as she tried to make sense of the impossible sight before her. Was he real? A deranged escapee? Panic surged through her veins, and she let out a bloodcurdling scream, the sound echoing off the walls. Desperate for protection, she frantically scanned the room, her trembling hand landing on the first object she could find: a wine bottle near her bedside table.

Clutching the bottle like a makeshift weapon, she charged toward the intruder, adrenaline overriding her fear. But as she approached, the figure remained unnervingly still, his gaze unbroken. Just as she was about to clock the man over the head with the bottle, he evaporated into thin air, leaving nothing but suffocating silence and her own terrified reflection in the window.

Some say that in conjunction with the presence of slave spirits, there's also the ghost of a maid still making her rounds on the property with an unyielding dedication to her duties, attempting to provide warmth and comfort in a world where she no longer belongs. If you can believe it, one occupant, deep in slumber, was stirred awake by the sensation of sheets being tugged under and around them. Blinking groggily in the dim room, they were horrified when they honed in on a ghostly woman, clad in an old-fashioned uniform, leaning over them as she proceeded to make the bed with the guest still in it. Such encounters with the spectral maid, who silently traverses the hotel from room to room, make a chilling impression on the hotel's staff and its guests. This unsettling phenomenon was not lost on Amanda Laing, who experienced a similar eerie sensation when she stayed at the Omni Royal Orleans Hotel in the summer of 2023.

Amanda was excited to be in New Orleans for her company's annual conference. After checking in to the hotel and being greeted by welcoming staff, Amanda settled into her room, unaware of the spectral experiences that awaited her.

Her first night was uneventful until the clock struck midnight. Amanda, lying in bed, heard a faint humming, a sound she dismissed as another guest's late-night activity. However, when she heard a distinct tap on her door, followed by taps near the bathroom and, finally, by her bed, her curiosity turned to unease. Trying to ignore it, she turned over, only to feel the pressure of something pressing against her at the bottom of the bed. It felt as though someone was tucking in the sheets or sitting on the edge of the bed. Amanda's heart raced, but she managed to fall asleep, attributing the experience to exhaustion.

The next morning, she joined her colleagues for the conference. As she began her presentation, an inexplicable technical glitch occurred: her slides began auto-advancing despite not being programmed to do so. Baffled, Amanda managed to finish her presentation, but the incident lingered in her mind.

That night, back in her room, the disturbances escalated. As she tried to relax, the television began changing channels on its own, mirroring the odd behavior of her presentation slides. The tapping noises returned, more persistent this time, and again, the pressure on the bed made her feel like an invisible entity was present.

Unable to relax or sleep, Amanda approached the front desk, recounting her eerie experiences. The staff, maintaining their professional composure, listened attentively. Without flinching, they accommodated her request for a room change, ensuring she felt as comfortable as possible.

The following day, Amanda learned she wasn't alone in her encounters. A coworker, equally startled, had also heard the mysterious humming during the night. The staff's calm and helpful demeanor provided some reassurance, but the haunting presence consumed Amanda's thoughts. Her stay at the Omni Royal Orleans Hotel was certainly unforgettable due to the ghostly encounters that left her questioning the boundary between the living and the dead.

In addition to the spirits, a subtle remnant of the St. Louis Hotel's dark history lingers at the property, thanks to preservation architect Samuel Wilson Jr., who managed to incorporate a fragment of the old "Exchange" sign used to advertise auctions. If you look up at the Chartres side of the Omni Royal Orleans Hotel, you'll see the word "Change" faintly etched above the columns near the parking garage, a symbolic reminder of the past and a call for societal improvement. This subtle sign encourages us to reflect on our values, look beyond appearances and strive for a future where compassion and equality prevail.

Though the faded inscription serves as a poignant reminder of past wrongs and a call for progress, the slave trade is only one fragment of the hotel's dark history. The Omni Royal Orleans Hotel's property, with its history of unsettling events, seems to be a magnet for societal atrocities. This dark reputation was further cemented by a deeply troubling incident culminating in twenty-eight-year-old Zackery "Zack" Bowen leaping to his death from the top of the building on October 17, 2006.

At about eight thirty in the evening, Detective Tom Morovic was on his way to grab some grub when a call came across his radio revealing that a man was lying dead on the rooftop of the parking garage of the Omni Royal Orleans Hotel. The New Orleans Police Department rushed to the scene, which was not for the faint of heart. Bowen had landed face down on the concrete, and the impact of the fall left his body in a horrific state, with blunt force trauma to his face and grotesquely twisted limbs. The officers immediately called the coroner, who showed up soon after, and they began their investigation. They searched Bowen's body for identification, noting twenty-eight small circular burns from cigarettes scattered across his skin like a constellation of pain. Trying to identify Bowen, they searched his pants pockets, and there they found a small plastic bag containing military dog tags revealing Bowen's full name and a folded-up letter that was labeled "For police only." As the officers opened and read the note, their expressions shifted from confusion to sheer horror as they absorbed the macabre details. An excerpt read:

> *This is not accidental. I had to take my own life to pay for the one I took. If you send a patrol car to 826 N. Rampart you will find the dismembered corpse of my girlfriend Addie in the oven, on the stove, and in the fridge along with full documentation on the both of us and a full signed confession from myself. The keys in my right front pocket are for the gates. Call Leo Watermeier to let you in. Zack Bowen.*

His suicide letter also revealed that the twenty-eight cigarette burns on his body were self-inflicted, each representing a year of his life that he considered a failure.

While law enforcement handled the crime scene at the hotel and beelined for the apartment (which can now be visited through Bloody Mary's Haunted Museum, where offerings may be left for the spirits), hotel staff reviewed the chilling surveillance footage that showed a wasted Bowen, who had been pounding drinks at the hotel's rooftop terrace bar, stumbling toward the ledge several times with hesitation before downing his final glass of liquor for liquid courage and throwing himself over the edge.

As investigators, including Detective Morovic, ascended the stairs and entered the small apartment on this balmy fall night, they were immediately struck by a blast of cold air. The biting chill was jarring in comparison to the warmth outside, and they soon realized the air conditioner was set to sixty degrees Fahrenheit. Their first view was of the living room walls, which were covered in spray-painted messages revealing blatant signs of Zack's severe psychological break. Phrases such as "Look in the oven," "Total failure," "I loved her," "Please help me stop the pain!!!" "I'm such a loser" and "Call Lana Bowen (wife)" were scrawled all over in large, bold letters. Horrified, Morovic entered the kitchen, bracing himself for the grisly sight that awaited him. Inside the tiny kitchen, a large arrow marked "Look" pointed toward the front of the oven, where "Don't look" was written, in contradiction. A covered stainless-steel pot sat ominously on one of the stovetop burners. Morovic's stomach churned in revulsion when he lifted the lid off the pot.

Inside was the decapitated head of thirty-year-old Adriane "Addie" Hall, cooked beyond recognition. Her hair and skin had peeled back from her skull in the extreme heat. Behind it, another pot contained Addie's severed hands and feet, which had been boiled, their appearance as appalling as it was shocking. Chopped carrots and potatoes were laid out nearby. The oven's contents were no less horrifying: a large disposable turkey pan held Addie's charred arms and legs, seasoned with herbs, as if Bowen had been preparing for a cannibalistic feast. This, however, was not the case: Bowen planned only to cook down her body to make it easier to dispose of. An autopsy of Zack's body disclosed that he had not, in fact, ingested any human remains, despite numerous rumors suggesting otherwise, which led to his being unfairly labeled the Cannibal of New Orleans.

Morovic felt the urge to leave the apartment but instead turned his attention to the refrigerator, where he found Addie's torso packed in a large black garbage bag. The tub where Bowen had dismembered Addie was eerily clean, indicating he'd attempted to meticulously scrub away the evidence of his dastardly deed. However, after he washed all her blood down the drain, he spray-painted the shower wall with the words, "I'm sorry I couldn't finish." Morovic's last and maybe worst discovery of all was Addie's journal, in which Zack detailed everything, starting with how he killed her. It featured the following confession:

Right: The oven and stovetop where Addie's severed body parts were discovered. *Author photo*.

Below: The bathtub where Zack dismembered Addie. *Author photo.*

> *Today is the 16th of October at 2:00 am. I killed her at 1:00 am on Thursday, October 5th. I very calmly strangled her. It was very quick. Halfway through the task, I stopped and thought about what I was doing. The decision to halt the first idea and move to Plan B, which is the crime scene you are now in, came after a while. I scared myself, not by the action of calmly strangling the woman I've loved for one and a half years and then desecrating her body, but my entire lack of remorse. I've known for forever how horrible a person I am. Ask anyone. And I decided to quit my jobs and spend the $1,500 cash I had being happy until I killed myself. So that's what I did. Good food, good drugs, good strippers, good friends, and any loose ends I may have had. I didn't contact any of my family, so that'll explain the shock. And had a fantastic time living out my days. It's just about time now.*

The journal continued with the abhorrent sequence of events, such as Zack's gross mistreatment and violation of Addie's dead body, driven by fury and lust. After asphyxiating Addie, Zack engaged in acts of necrophilia with her corpse on the futon, eventually passing out beside her, heavily intoxicated. The following morning, his mind was consumed with thoughts of how to get rid of her body. For the next few days, Zack did not show up for work and was unreachable. After Addie's body began to decompose in the sweltering Louisiana heat, he cranked the thermostat down and dragged it into the bathtub, where he proceeded to cut off Addie's head and limbs with a handsaw and a knife. He also chopped her hair off before placing her head in the pot on the stove. For the next twelve days, he went about his daily routine as if nothing was amiss as Addie's mutilated remains slowly decayed in the apartment.

How on earth did it ever come to this?

In 1995, a teenage Bowen took a road trip with his dad across the country. One of their stops was New Orleans. When his dad was ready to leave the city and go back to their home in Bakersfield, California, Bowen refused to go with him and stayed behind, claiming the Big Easy as his new home. As a good-looking and charismatic young man with a quick wit, Zack quickly found a new beginning in the vibrant nightlife of New Orleans' French Quarter.

Heavily immersed in the party scene, Zack eventually met a stripper named Lana Shupack, with whom he became enamored. Their relationship progressed rather quickly, leading to Lana becoming pregnant with their first child together. Unfortunately, Lana was in her late twenties when they met and was not aware that Zack was underage. As soon as Lana found out how young Zack was, she dumped him out of guilt, but she decided to follow through with her pregnancy, allowing Zack to be involved in the child's life only if he wanted it. Zack was too in love with Lana to leave her struggling as a single mother and expressed the desire for them to function as a family unit. Shortly thereafter, Zack proposed, and the couple got married when Zack was nineteen years old. Zack's mother disapproved of the age gap and was disappointed in the path her son had taken in his life, shedding many tears over what she believed to be a series of irresponsible decisions that would ruin his life and compromise his dreams. This was not at all what she had in mind for his future, and she knew these life-changing events would cause struggles for her son.

Sure enough, with the birth of Lana and Zack's second child in the spring of 2000, the couple found themselves in a difficult situation. Desperate to support his expanding household, Zack enlisted in the army. His skills quickly earned him promotions, leading to his role as a sergeant. For his distinguished service, he was honored with a NATO Medal and a Presidential Unit Citation. His deployments to Kosovo and Abu Ghraib in Iraq exposed him to intense and harrowing experiences. Among the most traumatic was witnessing the brutal murder of a small boy whom he had befriended. The child and his entire family were murdered by insurgents, targeted simply for interacting with American troops. This, along with the loss of his best friend, a fellow soldier who died in a car bombing, profoundly impacted Zack, leading to severe PTSD—a condition he did not have before his military service. When he returned to the United States, he carried the weight of these traumas, compounded by the disappointment of receiving a general discharge instead of the honorable one his commanding officer had recommended. This discharge left him disillusioned and bitter. On returning to New Orleans, his personality had totally changed; he was emotionally withdrawn and showed a lack of empathy that scared his wife. The person she fell in love with was no longer present. Because of this, their once loving marriage fell apart, and when their divorce was finalized, Zack was left alone, struggling with the trauma of his experiences and a deep sense of inadequacy.

By the summer of 2005, twenty-seven-year-old Zack seemed to have mastered the art of suppressing his PTSD and outwardly appeared confident and carefree. About six months after coming back to the city, he found a job working the graveyard shift at a bar where crowds of people would come to see him perform magic tricks. His newfound swagger drew the ladies to him like moths to a flame, while men thought he was the epitome of cool. He was adored by almost everyone he crossed paths with, none of them aware of the storm quietly building inside him.

Despite all the attention Zack received, he was solely focused on Addie, an artsy, free-spirited, bohemian bartender whose shifts began as his ended. Initially, Addie was one of the few who were not impressed by Bowen at all, thinking he was too rigid in his beliefs and mannerisms from his military past and thrown off by what she perceived as insincerity. One day, Bowen, who was determined to win her over, waited for her to get out of work and offered up shots of Jägermeister for them to enjoy together. Both regular drinkers and casual drug users, they quickly bonded over their shared love for partying, and that eventually extended into sharing other parts of their lives, too. Bowen began confiding in his mother that he had found the love of his life and referred to Addie as his soulmate. Everyone around them thought they were an adorable couple and could see just how smitten he was with her by the way he gazed at her. Despite such shows of affection, it was almost as if Zack had another life altogether. He tended to hide significant aspects of his past from Addie and their friends, including the fact that he was previously married and had children with Lana. When Addie found out about Zack's past, she exploded in anger, but ultimately, she decided she loved him and really wanted to make it work.

When Lana got wind that Hurricane Katrina was about to hit, she begged Zack to come to her and be with her and their kids, but he refused, opting to stay with Addie instead in her French Quarter apartment in a bold attempt to ride out the storm, turning the impending disaster into a frenzied romantic adventure.

After withstanding the storm unharmed, the couple was viewed as heroic and gained media attention for assisting others in need; their unconventional survival tactics, including trading drinks for essentials; and Addie's infamous antics, like flashing police officers. In the aftermath of the storm, they didn't have to pay any bills or have any responsibilities and could do whatever they wanted, whenever they wanted in the primarily empty French Quarter. They grilled, drank themselves into oblivion, had sex on the streets and partied from dawn until dusk, with no access to technology and no expectation of having to answer to a boss. When TV crews finally showed up to film, Bowen used a crew member's cell phone to ring his mother and let her know everything was okay.

For weeks, Lana desperately searched for Zack, fearing the worst and convinced he might be injured or dead. Her anxiety grew until, finally, she

Zack Bowen and Addie Hall in the French Quarter after Hurricane Katrina, looking very much in love. *Courtesy of IMAGO/ZUMA Press Wire.*

found his name on the Red Cross website and discovered the truth. Zack wasn't injured or missing; he was out barbecuing and enjoying drinks, caught up in his own world, Lana's fears and the well-being of his children not even a blip on his radar as he failed to reach out with any news.

As the city began to return to normal, the bubble of Zack and Addie's newfound existence started to burst. The couple was unprepared to go back to the way things were, and as a result, their post-Katrina euphoria was short-lived. Their relationship began deteriorating under the strain of parental responsibilities, heavy drinking, drug use, Addie's uncontrollable temper and Zack's PTSD.

A month after Hurricane Katrina, Zack finally reached out to Lana, who had been coping alone with their two kids and was feeling furious, overwhelmed and unsupported. They met at a local bar, where Zack admitted to his mistakes and they agreed on shared custody: he would have the children every other weekend. Despite this compromise, Addie resented Lana's influence over their arrangement. As life began to return to its routine, the cracks in Zack and Addie's relationship started to show.

Desperate for money, Zack took a mundane job at a grocery store, while Addie began bartending, where she found enjoyment in dancing atop the bar, much to the delight of her male patrons, who showered her in hefty tips. One night, when Zack came into the bar and saw this occur, he exploded into a fit of rage and jealousy at Addie's display, leading to a confrontation with her. Addie's manager, Eura Jones, tried to explain to Zack that Addie was loyal to him and was only trying to earn a living and keep the customers happy, but Zack remained unsatisfied. His controlling behavior and lack of trust caused their relationship to deteriorate further. What was once casual drug use between the couple soon escalated into full-blown addiction. Zack's unresolved trauma, which haunted him relentlessly, certainly didn't help, and his worsening addiction drove him further off the deep end.

To retaliate against Addie, Zack started having one-night stands. Addie, frustrated by his persistent jealousy, confided to her friends that she was considering leaving him. During one particularly heated night of drinking and playing games, an argument erupted into violence, and Zack hit her for the first time—a troubling precursor to more violence. The following morning, Zack announced to his friends that he was leaving New Orleans and Addie behind and purchased a train ticket to the state of Washington. On waking up, Addie found his departure note and was heartbroken. The next day at work, when asked about her bruises, she revealed they were the result of Zack's aggression, explaining that their fights turned physical when they were intoxicated. But the pain of their separation was intense, and Zack began to reconsider his decision. Their frequent phone conversations made it clear that they felt they needed to reunite. After a brief separation, Zack returned to the Crescent City and to Addie, a decision that would ultimately lead to disastrous consequences.

Just two days after reuniting, Zack and Addie fell back into their old habits, indulging in heavy drinking and drug use. Their relationship, already unstable, deteriorated further as their arguments became more intense and violent. One night, during a particularly heated dispute, Addie locked Zack out of the apartment. Desperate and furious, Zack pounded on the door, alarming a nearby neighbor and prompting a police call. Zack was briefly arrested but quickly released.

The turbulent relationship, characterized by a constant cycle of breaking up and reconciling, became increasingly toxic. In retaliation for being locked out, Zack began a relationship with another man, revealing his bisexuality to Addie for the first time. Although Zack had openly shared his bisexuality with friends, he had kept this part of himself hidden from Addie, who was vocal about her homophobia. Deeply offended and repulsed by this revelation, Addie viewed it as the ultimate betrayal.

Amid their turmoil, Addie had gotten into an argument with the landlord at her previous unit and so she and Zack moved into a tiny apartment located above Priestess Miriam's Voodoo Spiritual Temple. To pay for the deposit and the move, Zack worked several jobs nearly around the clock. Despite his financial efforts, Addie wanted to punish Zack for what he'd done, and she was sick of the constant bickering between them. Having had enough, on October 4, 2006, Addie visited their landlord to ask for a change to their lease, hoping to eliminate Zack's name and legally expel him from the apartment. The landlord suggested she discuss the matter with Zack rather than proceeding with the modification. This advice proved to be deadly.

The situation reached a breaking point when Addie, consumed by rage, began hurling Zack's belongings out of their apartment during an aggressive outburst. She publicly humiliated him, using his bisexuality and infidelity as weapons to further wound him. In a moment of desperation, to get her to be quiet, Zack wrapped his hands around her neck in a final, and fatal, attempt to silence her. Initially horrified by his actions and faced with the shock of his own brutality, he contemplated fleeing but ultimately decided to stay and pen the blow-by-blow account in a cocaine-fueled haze, tragically stating that he still loved her.

When mutual friends began inquiring about Addie, noticing her unusual silence and absence, Zack always had a good excuse to cover his tracks. In fact, after killing Addie, Zack contacted several friends, telling them that she had finally left him for good and moved home to North Carolina. Given Addie's spontaneous nature, her friends dismissed any suspicions they may have had. When Zack finally appeared, his friends noticed that he looked disheveled and unshaven, clearly having been on a prolonged bender. People who knew him thought he was acting funny, too. His mom went an extended period without hearing from him, and then Zack called Lana, saying he wanted to party with her. She refused to go, and that was the last time she ever heard from him. Instead, Zack invited Addie's best friend, Capricho De Vellas, to come party with him. This would be the night Zack would commit suicide, but Capricho thought Zack seemed like his normal, jovial self that night. Zack treated Capricho to lap dances and drinks. When Capricho finally departed from their guys' night out, Zack retired alone to the Omni Royal Orleans Hotel, where he took his last breath.

Although they're exceedingly controversial, there have been reports of a male spirit resembling Zack Bowen seen at La Riviera. This tall, strong figure with sandy hair drifts through the bar with an unsettling familiarity. He doesn't interact with anyone, nor does he give off any air of otherworldliness. Instead, he paces by the bar's ledge, occasionally glancing over it as if reliving his grueling final moments, lost in his own world. To the casual observer, he might seem like just another reveler, but those familiar with his story recognize him instantly.

The most unsettling aspect of this apparition is his sudden, inexplicable vanishing. He doesn't fade or shimmer out of sight; he simply disappears. One moment he's there, and the next he's gone—disappearing as suddenly as if he had never been there at all. It appears as if Zack Bowen's spirit is trapped in a perpetual loop, endlessly reliving his final moments. His spectral form wanders the bar, repeatedly reenacting his last actions in a ceaseless cycle.

The story of Zack and Addie is yet another somber chapter that partially unfolded on the hotel's grounds. Although it was one of the most heinous crimes ever committed in New Orleans and across the country, it brings to light the importance of recognizing and addressing the critical issue of untreated mental illness, particularly among veterans. It highlights the severe consequences of neglecting mental health challenges, often compounded by shame and societal stigma, and how such neglect can deeply affect a person's well-being and coping mechanisms. The story also draws attention to violence in all its forms—emotional, sexual, mental, verbal and physical abuse—and the warning signs associated with it. By examining our own relationships, whether familial, platonic or romantic, we can learn to identify red flags in seemingly normal situations to prevent them from escalating into tragic outcomes. This story serves as a powerful reminder to foster greater empathy and understanding toward one another. Since their lives were lost in such unfathomable ways, it should come as no surprise that those haunting the Omni Royal Orleans Hotel aren't quite able to rest in peace. It is my hope that one day, they will find the solace they so desperately seek.

CHAPTER 7

BIDDING ADIEU TO LITTLE BOY BLUE

HOTEL MONTELEONE
214 ROYAL STREET
NEW ORLEANS, LOUISIANA 70130

One of my favorite themes in the New Orleans–inspired Disney film *The Princess and the Frog* is the idea that anyone, with enough hard work and perseverance, can build a life doing what they love in a city that they love. This was certainly true for Antonio Monteleone, a Sicilian-born cobbler, who immigrated to New Orleans during the 1880s with plans to eventually open a shoe factory. As he forged his path in the Big Easy, he could not have predicted that his achievements would lay the groundwork for a legacy interwoven with both grandeur and ghostly whispers—earning the present-day hotel a spot on *USA Today*'s 2024 Readers' Choice Awards list of the Top 10 Best Haunted Hotels in America, where it ranks no. 8.

Monteleone's journey began with a modest shoe store at the intersection of Saint Louis and Royal Streets. As his business began to thrive, he relocated to a larger location at the junction of Conti and Royal. Eventually, he rented a building on the corner of Bienville and Royal, located just across from an unassuming hotel that caught his interest and sparked his imagination.

In 1886, Antonio Monteleone purchased the sixty-four-room hotel at the corner of Royal and Iberville Streets initially built as the Hotel Victor and later renamed the Commercial Hotel. Monteleone acquired it under this name before purchasing neighboring lots and embarking on extensive renovations over the years to accommodate more guests. In the early twentieth century, its name would be changed once again. Monteleone cleverly integrated his shoe business into the hotel by situating the store and factory on the ground

The Hotel Monteleone's doors are believed to not only welcome the living but also confine the spirits of those who never left. *Courtesy of Amy Shabluk.*

floor while reserving the upper floors for hotel rooms. This innovative approach was highly successful, especially since Royal Street was a bustling center of commerce and banking at the time. Under Antonio's management, the hotel grew steadily in size and popularity, eagerly welcoming an unstoppable stream of patrons, which allowed Monteleone to provide a comfortable living for his wife, Sophia, and their children.

A plaque on the wall of the Hotel Monteleone's lobby commemorates Antonio Monteleone, the hotel's founder. *Courtesy of Amy Shabluk.*

A few legends still circulate about one of the first families to stay at the hotel when it was under Monteleone's ownership. The original legend has it that in the 1890s, Jacques and Josephine Begere, along with their three-year-old toddler, Maurice, checked into the Commercial Hotel and were assigned Room 1462 on the fourteenth floor (which is actually the thirteenth floor). Enthusiastic theatregoers, they often visited the French Opera House for date nights. One evening, while the Begeres indulged in a night at the opera, they left young Maurice in the care of a nanny.

That night, Maurice came down with a wicked illness. Once a lively and energetic child, he was now wracked with a fever that seemed to consume his small body. His vibrant eyes, usually filled with curiosity, were clouded and vacant. He lay motionless in his bed, his skin burning with an unnatural heat as he whimpered weakly. The fever's grip tightened, rendering him a shadow of his former self, and his cries for comfort were extremely heartrending. The fever continued to rage, and soon Maurice's tiny frame was seized by a series of violent convulsions, each more harrowing than the last. As the hours slipped away into the deepening night, a stillness settled over his room, a quiet so profound it seemed to whisper of an unimaginable loss.

When Jacques and Josephine returned from their evening out, the joy of their night was abruptly shattered. They were met with the devastating sight of their beloved son lying in bed, lifeless and cold. The weight of their grief was unbearable, and they fell to their knees as their hearts shattered into pieces. Their cries, a haunting mixture of heartbreak and disbelief, were so powerful that they reached every room on the floor.

In the years that followed, Jacques and Josephine returned to the fourteenth floor of the hotel every year on the anniversary of Maurice's death, driven by an unrelenting hope to reconnect with their lost child. Thankfully, it didn't take them long to connect with Maurice's spirit, and he finally made an appearance before his mourning mother. In a spectral vision, Maurice's wispy form, pale and tiny, appeared and said, "*Maman, ne pleure pas. Je vais bien.*" ("Mommy, don't cry. I'm fine.") The sighting left Josephine both sad and profoundly relieved, knowing her child was at peace.

However, an alternate legend presents a different account. While some say Maurice stayed at the hotel with his parents, there are claims that he did not die there. Instead, the story suggests he passed away off-site but returned to the hotel as a ghost, searching for his parents. In this version, Maurice's father, Jacques, tragically lost his life on the way back to the hotel after a night at the opera while riding in a carriage. Apparently, the horse got spooked by a loud, unexpected sound and charged forward, hurling Jacques to the ground, where he was killed on impact. Josephine, overcome with grief, died of a broken heart within a year of losing both her husband and son. Some even claim that Maurice did not die as a child at all. Instead, he lived on as an orphan, having lost both his parents at a very young age, and returned to the hotel in death as a child, desperately searching for the parents he lost.

Whatever you believe pertaining to the legends, it's apparent that a young boy still roams the old hotel, because over the years, hundreds of people have reported encounters with his ghost. He is often seen playing on the fourteenth floor, and his childlike giggles can be heard throughout the hotel when the city finally settles in to fall asleep.

One visitor recounted a particularly unsettling experience where she was awakened in the early hours of the morning by a small, ghostly figure walking past the foot of her bed. The apparition, believed to be the ghost of Maurice, moved silently yet left a trail of cold air in its wake. Panicked, the guest bolted upright to get a better look at the figure and tell her husband about it, only to realize he was not in the room and she was alone. As I'm sure you might have guessed, this began happening to other guests as well and now has become a regular occurrence. So when you stay at this hotel, you might want to keep your feet tucked securely under the covers to avoid any unexpected playful touches.

Cheryl Bananno had been living in New Orleans for nearly a decade when, in 2021, she was offered a position as a host at the Carousel Bar and Criollo Restaurant inside the Hotel Monteleone. She saw this as a fantastic employment opportunity, but she was unaware it would introduce her to the world of the supernatural.

While working at the Hotel Monteleone, Cheryl noticed unusual activity involving the elevator, such as unexplained stops and irregularities, a common phenomenon that many attribute to Maurice's playful ghost. It is said that when children ride the elevator, they are taken to the fourteenth floor regardless of what button they push. However, many adults have reported experiencing the same thing, so it's safe to say that this is not an experience reserved only for kids.

In another instance, a photograph shared with Cheryl, taken in the dimly lit hallway of the fourteenth floor, captured an unmistakably clear silhouette of a child standing against the wall across from the ice machine sign. This shadowy figure is believed to be the physical manifestation of Maurice.

Although Maurice's rumored death has literally shadowed the halls, the hotel's success continued to flourish, paving the way for significant growth and transformation. By 1902, Antonio Monteleone had seized an opportunity to expand the hotel's footprint by acquiring additional property on Exchange Alley, enhancing the Commercial Hotel greatly. This expansion was a prelude to even more ambitious plans.

In 1905, the hotel was officially renamed the Hotel Monteleone, a nod to its proud new ownership and rising prominence in New Orleans. By 1908, the hotel's increasing popularity had necessitated a major overhaul, prompting Antonio Monteleone to invest $260,000 in a comprehensive rebuild and expansion. The newly designed building became one of three Beaux Arts–style structures in New Orleans, marking a significant architectural achievement.

However, this large renovation was just the beginning. The hotel underwent five major expansions over the years, some of which were overseen by Antonio's son, Frank, who took over the property in 1913, after his fifty-eight-year-old father died while en route to Germany. At the time of this book's publication, the Hotel Monteleone has been owned by five generations of the Monteleone family and is one of many family-run hotels still operating in the United States today. Among the notable expansions, 1949's saw the elimination of the hotel's lounge, the Swan Room, and the

Above: A postcard from the early 1900s featuring the newly rebranded Hotel Monteleone. *Public domain.*

Opposite: The sign outside of the Hotel Monteleone. *Courtesy of Jacob Walker, New Orleans Portrait Photography.*

debut of the Carousel Piano Bar & Lounge, which is still the centerpiece of the hotel today. This unique addition features 186 twinkling lights and twenty-five carousel seats, each intricately hand-painted. What's even more exciting is that the carousel itself gracefully completes a full circuit every fifteen minutes, drawing locals and tourists from all over the world to share a drink at one of the most unique bars in the United States. A-list celebrities often frequent this bar as well, so if you visit, be sure to keep your eyes peeled. You never know who you might meet!

In 1954, the hotel experienced another transformative renovation, replacing the original building with a new structure that included expanded guestrooms, ballrooms, dining rooms and cocktail lounges. This extensive update was followed by the final significant expansion, in 1964, which introduced more guestrooms and added a luxurious Sky Terrace complete with a large pool and upscale cocktail lounge. The hotel's ongoing changes created even more public interest, and it soon became a creative haven for literary greats, attracting some of the most celebrated writers of the twentieth century.

Literary giants such as Truman Capote, Ernest Hemingway, Tennessee Williams, Eudora Welty, William Faulkner, Sherwood Anderson, Anne Rice and Lyle Saxon frequented the Hotel Monteleone and drew inspiration from within its walls. In 1999, its literary significance was officially recognized when it was designated a national literary landmark by the Friends of the Library Association. To date, the hotel has appeared as a setting in over 173 publications!

Despite its reputation as a gathering place for literary legends, more than one tale set at the Hotel Monteleone whispers of despair and finality. On October 27, 1942, Innis Patterson, a talented New Orleans–born writer who had been involved with the Federal Writers' Project, found herself at the edge of a different kind of narrative, one marked by personal turmoil and tragic fate. Patterson, who had once dedicated herself to writing compelling works of art, became the subject of her own tragic story.

Overwhelmed by grief and mental anguish, Innis ascended to her room on the twelfth floor of the Hotel Monteleone and locked herself inside. She had registered there only a few days earlier, awaiting a permanent housing arrangement following the suicide of her husband, George Wolf III, the previous Christmas. The loss of George left her bereft and increasingly despondent. By her bed, sleeping tablets were found, hinting at her attempts to find solace or escape from her overwhelming pain, but it was obvious that nothing could stop the agonizing depression she felt.

Earlier that day, she spent time in Jackson Square with her friend Mrs. H. Sherman Baker, who noticed her profound sadness. When they parted ways around two thirty in the afternoon, Mrs. Baker observed that Innis appeared deeply troubled. By six o'clock, the city below Innis's hotel window was bustling with peak traffic, oblivious to the tragedy unfolding above.

In a final, desperate act, Innis opened one of the windows in her room and cut out an opening in the screen before stepping through. As she fell, the city's sounds were momentarily drowned out by the rush of air and the violent force of her descent. The impact was catastrophic. Her body struck the pavement with a sickening thud, narrowly missing the cars that sped by during rush hour. Her skull was fractured on impact, and the force of the fall caused her limbs to shatter entirely, all at once. The severe trauma resulted in immediate hemorrhage and shock.

Passersby witnessed the horrifying scene as Innis's body lay mangled on the street, and she was quickly rushed to Charity Hospital, where her death was pronounced shortly afterward, attributed to the extensive injuries she sustained.

Mrs. Baker helped confirm Innis's identity. She described how her friend had been increasingly dejected since George's death and recalled their final moments together. The note Innis left behind, though only partially legible, expressed her gratitude to Mrs. Baker and conveyed her profound sorrow. "I loved him, how much you'll never know," she wrote, a final testament to her enduring love and overwhelming grief.

Lyle Saxon, a fellow writer and contemporary, later reflected on the tragedy in a letter. He recounted the unfortunate nature of Innis's death and noted an unsettling sense of inevitability. Saxon had been aware of Innis's previous attempts to end her life: she had tried to poison herself in a manner similar to the way George ended his life and also attempted to slash her wrists. His reflections highlighted the depth of Innis's inner torment and the tragic culmination of her struggles. With the world continuing its course, Innis chose to leave her pain behind, along with her soul.

As evening settles over the hotel, guests on the twelfth floor begin their nightly routines: getting comfortable, preparing for dinner or heading out to explore the French Quarter. However, their preparations are often interrupted by an unnerving sight: fleeting glimpses of a spectral figure, its head hovering just outside the windowpane.

The figure appears only for a moment, but it's distinct enough to leave an impression. Witnesses describe a ghostly visage—with short, wavy dark hair and a thin, somber face—peering in from the other side of the glass. Many believe the spirit resembles Innis Patterson as she was in life.

The sight is chilling and deeply unsettling, as if she is searching for something—or someone. Some guests swear they can feel her eyes pressing against the window, watching every move they make. Given the extensive history of hauntings at the Hotel Monteleone, it's no wonder that Innis Patterson, and others like her, still linger on the property.

Innis Patterson. *Courtesy of the New Orleans Item.*

A paranormal investigation conducted in March 2003 by the International Society of Paranormal Research uncovered far more spirits than the well-known presence of Maurice. Alongside the young boy, the team made contact with at least twelve other spirits, many of whom were former staff members or had other connections to the hotel. Among these spirits is William Wilder, a name associated with a man who passed away in the early twentieth century. His ghost is said to haunt the fourteenth floor, where he spent much of his time, and is rumored to keep Maurice company there. His ghostly figure is described as moving purposefully down the hallways, accompanied by the eerie sound of his scuffling footsteps as he makes his way from room to room, still managing tasks or attending to unfinished business.

Cheryl Bananno believes she encountered one of those other souls. While working one day at the host stand, she felt a gentle pat on the side of her head. Believing it to be a playful gesture from a coworker, she reached up to reciprocate the affection, only to find that no one was there.

Many of Cheryl's colleagues have also reported paranormal encounters. For example, a pastry chef who worked at the hotel for years frequently spoke of a mischievous little girl haunting the kitchen. On one occasion, sensing her presence nearby, the staff began taking photographs that, surprisingly, revealed a young girl in an old-fashioned dress alongside the chef. The little girl, who has been named Emilie, is another child rumored to have died on-site, this time in an elevator accident. Her spirit has been witnessed all over the property, but it seems she has quite an affinity for the kitchen or for the people that work within it.

A longtime pastry chef at the Hotel Monteleone sensed a presence, and when photos were taken, a young girl in period dress appeared alongside him, believed to be the spirit of Emilie. *Courtesy of Cheryl Bananno.*

Cheryl herself noted that while her experiences at the "Grand Dame of Royal Street" were intriguing rather than terrifying, the phenomenon was palpable. As she put it, "I have lived in New Orleans for eight years, and I assure you the veil is much thinner here."

Another spirit that appears frequently is sculptor Antonio Puccio, who hand-carved the hotel's antique mahogany grandfather clock specifically for the Hotel Monteleone back in 1909. He's an inconspicuous figure, dressed in old-timey clothing, his head bowed as he intently inspects the timepiece. Most passersby don't think twice about it—after all, an old clock like that requires maintenance. But those who stop to watch longer, or happen to walk past him, notice something strange: he never seems to leave.

Those who have seen him describe the same details—a hunched-over figure donning spectacles and wearing a waistcoat. Some say his presence is calming, while others feel a chill when they pass by the clock, noting that it's

This beautiful hand-carved grandfather clock is purportedly haunted by its sculptor, Antonio Puccio. *Courtesy of Amy Shabluk.*

always unusually cold in that section of the lobby when he's around, even in the blistering summer heat.

So if you ever find yourself in the Hotel Monteleone's lobby, take a moment to glance at the clock. You might just see Antonio Puccio there—still perfecting his craft, even in death.

The Hotel Monteleone is not only a place to stay but also an experience to be savored. As you settle into your luxurious room and take in the stunning ambiance of this historic gem, don't miss the chance to grab drinks at the Carousel Bar. Go for a spin while sipping on a Vieux Carré, the famed cocktail crafted by head bartender Walter Bergeron in 1938. This signature drink honors the diverse culture of New Orleans, blending cognac for the French, rye whiskey for the Americans, sweet vermouth for the Italians and bitters for the Caribbeans. And of course, when your stay finally comes to an end, be sure to take a moment to bid adieu to Maurice and farewell to the other souls who call Hotel Monteleone home.

CHAPTER 8

CLEAN BEDS, DREAD AND BLOODSHED

THE HAUNTED HOTEL
623 URSULINES AVENUE
NEW ORLEANS, LOUISIANA 70116

You've heard of the likes of Jeffrey Dahmer, Ted Bundy, John Wayne Gacy, Aileen Wuornos, Richard Ramirez, Ed Gein and Albert Fish, but have you heard of the Axeman? Whenever I ask folks this question, I am stunned by the amount of people who tell me they've never heard of him, as he was one of the most abominable serial killers in New Orleans' history. In the early part of the twentieth century, he terrorized the whole city before wreaking havoc on those residing in Gretna, mainly targeting Italian grocers, who often lived in apartments or homes attached to their stores.

His plan of attack was always very similar. After seeking out his victims, he would approach their home in the depths of the night, first chiseling into the door panel to pry it loose—just enough to reach in and quietly unlock the door from the inside. Other times, he would use a common burglary tool known as a railroad shoe pin. Once inside, he crept toward the master bedroom, where his victims lay asleep. Grabbing an axe owned by those he was about to attack, he swung with terrifying force, the blade cleaving through flesh and bone, sending blood splattering across the room. The victims, caught while asleep, stood no chance. Those who did catch a glimpse of the intruder in their final moments saw a large man, approximately in his thirties, garbed in a slouch hat and dark-colored suit. He wasn't interested in material gain, only in the act of murder, leaving behind a horrific aftermath before disappearing without a trace: a blood-drenched hatchet with chunks of flesh and strands of hair still clinging to the blade. However, if a hatchet wasn't available, the Axeman had no qualms about using another instrument of murder, such as a straight razor or a butcher's knife.

Many believe the Axeman's reign of terror over New Orleans lasted from May 1918 to October 1919. However, according to an article in *Smithsonian Magazine*, his spree started back in 1917. But when it comes to the Axeman, there is far more to the story than what meets the eye. Based on my research from a collection of historical archives, it appears that his string of attacks could have begun as far back as 1910. Many unsolved killings starting around that time bear striking similarities to the Axeman's later murders: Italians were targeted, and the victims' own weapons were used against them.

On the muggy summer night of August 13, 1910, an intruder broke into the Crutti family's home at 4301 Royal Street, whacking August Crutti and his wife over the head with a meat cleaver. Shockingly, the pair survived the savage attack. The attacker then wandered barefoot from the scene; a neighbor reported seeing him leave the Crutti residence with their birdcage. He carried it a short distance away from their home before releasing their pet mockingbird into the wild. Then the strange man put on his shoes and escaped into the night.

On September 20, 1910, Joseph Risetto and his wife, who operated a grocery store out of their home, were brutally attacked by an unknown assailant. A small, size 4 shoe print found outside their residence led to speculation that the attacker might have been a woman. Meanwhile, John Feehan was arrested for attacking a woman with a knife on Canal Street and quickly earned the monikers Jack the Stabber and Jack the Slasher before being confined to a mental asylum. Despite his capture, the assaults did not cease.

In 1911, another horrific attack occurred in the Davi residence: Joe Davi and his sixteen-year-old wife, Marie, were also attacked with a meat cleaver. Joe was the first victim to die in this murder rampage, while Marie was gravely injured.

In May 1912, Anthony Sciambra was shot multiple times while asleep beside his wife, Johanna, who was also injured by the gunfire: the bullets that struck Anthony ended up hitting Johanna's hip. Their infant was also sleeping in bed with them but, luckily, remained unharmed. Johanna survived for ten days after the attack but ultimately died from her wounds. The assailant was never caught, and no arrests were made.

In 1914, a man was taken into custody for cutting the hair of several young girls. The incidents occurred while they were at the movies, on the

St. Charles streetcar and on their way to school. The *Daily Picayune* dubbed him Jack the Clipper.

On March 10, 1917, Vincent Miramon, a dairy farmer, was murdered, after being pummeled with a hammer. Although this murder did not involve an axe, Miramon was still categorized as a victim of the Axeman. One individual was arrested in connection with the crime, but no conviction was made.

Just three days prior to Christmas in 1917, Epifania Andollina, his wife and their two sons, who ran a grocery store, were assaulted with a hatchet in their home. Remarkably, all four survived the attack, though they sustained glancing blows. Despite the gravity of the situation, no arrests were made, and the case remained unresolved.

The killer's most infamous spree, however, began in 1918. On May 23, grocer Joseph Maggio and his wife, Catherine, were found dead in their home at 4901 Magnolia Street. Both had been attacked while they slept, their throats slit and their bodies further mutilated by being hacked up with an axe. Detectives discovered discarded clothes nearby, stained with blood, suggesting the killer changed before making his getaway. A straight razor, found on a neighbor's lawn, was traced back to Joseph's brother, Andrew Maggio, who ran a barbershop. Days before the murder, he took it home with him to repair its blade. Despite initial suspicions, Andrew was found innocent. Near the crime scene, however, a chilling message written in chalk stated: "Mrs. Joseph Maggio will sit up tonight. Just write Mrs. Toney."

On June 27, 1918, Louis Besumer and his mistress, Harriet Lowe, were attacked in their apartment, which also operated as a grocery store. The killer struck while they slept, using a hatchet that belonged to Besumer himself. Though both survived the assault, Lowe's injuries were severe. Like in the Maggio case, police found no signs of forced entry or robbery, and the weapon appeared to have come from inside the home. Once again, the mystery deepened.

On the night of August 5, 1918, the Axeman struck again. This time, Anna Schneider, a woman seven months pregnant, was attacked while sleeping in her bed. Her assailant bludgeoned her with a heavy bedside lamp. By way of a miracle, she survived the attack, although she could recall little of what happened, which was of no help in identifying the perpetrator. Five days later, Joseph Romano, an elderly man, was found by his nieces after sustaining severe head injuries from an axe. His nieces saw the fleeing attacker with their own eyes and described him to law enforcement. Romano later died from the extent of his injuries.

As the city was gripped by fear, the attacks continued. On March 10, 1919, the Axeman targeted Charles and Rosie Cortimiglia in their home in Gretna, just across the Mississippi River. Both were severely injured, and their infant daughter, tragically, did not survive. The attack was one of the most gut-wrenching in the Axeman's spree.

On August 10, 1919, Steve Bocca was viciously hacked by an axe in his bed. He wound up with severe injuries and, in a bloodied state, rushed to a neighbor's house to get help.

Then, almost a month later, on September 3, 1919, nineteen-year-old Sarah Laumann was assaulted while asleep, sustaining severe head injuries and losing all her teeth as a result of the trauma. The Axeman's terror continued. Thankfully, Laumann's piercing screams drove the attacker away.

The final killing occurred on October 27, 1919, when Mike Pepitone was murdered in his home. Unable to find an axe, the attacker used an iron bar, delivering fatal blows that left Pepitone's face severely disfigured: it was described in the *Times-Picayune* as an "unrecognizable mass." His wife, Esther, discovered him shortly after the incident, catching sight of the manslayer as he dashed off beneath the blackened sky.

William Carson, on the other hand, fired a gun at an intruder who may have been the Axeman, successfully scaring him away even though he missed. These assaults marked the end of the Axeman's spree, as no further attacks were reported.

Throughout his spree, the Axeman left the police and the public grasping for answers. The *Times-Picayune* fueled the city's terror, often dramatizing events and amplifying the fear that gripped New Orleans, although it really didn't need to—the true stories were, by far, horrific enough. Chaos really began to unfold when the *Times-Picayune* printed a letter that the Axeman supposedly penned to the people of New Orleans:

> *Hell, March 13, 1919*
> *Esteemed Mortal of New Orleans:*
>
> *They have never caught me and they never will. They have never seen me, for I am invisible, even as the ether that surrounds your earth. I am not a human being, but a spirit and a demon from the hottest hell. I am what you Orleanians and your foolish police call the Axeman.*
>
> *When I see fit, I shall come and claim other victims. I alone know whom they shall be. I shall leave no clue except my bloody axe, besmeared with blood and brains of he whom I have sent below to keep me company.*

If you wish you may tell the police to be careful not to rile me. Of course, I am a reasonable spirit. I take no offense at the way they have conducted their investigations in the past. In fact, they have been so utterly stupid as to not only amuse me, but His Satanic Majesty, Francis Josef, etc. But tell them to beware. Let them not try to discover what I am, for it were better that they were never born than to incur the wrath of the Axeman. I don't think there is any need of such a warning, for I feel sure the police will always dodge me, as they have in the past. They are wise and know how to keep away from all harm.

Undoubtedly, you Orleanians think of me as a most horrible murderer, which I am, but I could be much worse if I wanted to. If I wished, I could pay a visit to your city every night. At will I could slay thousands of your best citizens (and the worst), for I am in close relationship with the Angel of Death.

Now, to be exact, at 12:15 (earthly time) on next Tuesday night, I am going to pass over New Orleans. In my infinite mercy, I am going to make a little proposition to you people. Here it is:

I am very fond of jazz music, and I swear by all the devils in the nether regions that every person shall be spared in whose home a jazz band is in full swing at the time I have just mentioned. If everyone has a jazz band going, well, then, so much the better for you people. One thing is certain and that is that some of your people who do not jazz it out on that specific Tuesday night (if there be any) will get the axe.

Well, as I am cold and crave the warmth of my native Tartarus, and it is about time I leave your earthly home, I will cease my discourse. Hoping that thou wilt publish this, that it may go well with thee, I have been, am and will be the worst spirit that ever existed either in fact or realm of fancy.
—The Axeman

Not only were people scrambling in horror trying to gather instruments to play to appease the Axeman, but speculation about the Axeman's motives also began running rampant. Some believed his attacks were racially motivated, targeting Italian immigrants who were facing widespread discrimination in the United States at the time. Theories involving the Black Hand, or the Mafia, were briefly considered due to the Italian background of many victims, but these theories were rejected due to no corroborating evidence.

Another curious idea was that the Axeman's violence was tied to jazz music. Some speculated that he was exacting revenge for Black jazz musicians not getting due credit. After all, in 1917, the first jazz recording ever made was led by an Italian American musician, Dominic James "Nick" LaRocca, whose band, the Original Dixieland Jass Band (later spelled Jazz), stirred controversy by claiming to have "invented" jazz. Could the Axeman have been defending jazz's honor or retaliating for this cultural theft? Eric Hofbauer, jazz guitarist, composer and chair of the Jazz and Contemporary Music Department at Longy School of Music of Bard College, has discussed these theories, though he is skeptical of their validity.

There were other theories as well, such as the possibility that the killer was angered by the closure of Storyville. Storyville had been a hotbed for jazz, and its closure was a blow to the music scene. Others believed the Axeman might have simply been using his crimes to drum up attention for jazz music itself.

Thankfully, on the appointed Tuesday, every life in New Orleans was spared by the Axeman. While a good number of homes did have jazz music loudly blaring, most New Orleanians opted to get a good night's sleep, ignoring the serial killer's menacing threats.

Several suspects were examined during the Axeman investigation. Emmett Daniels, a World War I veteran, was charged with the 1917 murder of two women in Belgium and was also suspected of other crimes, but he was ultimately acquitted. James Gleason, a former convict, was briefly detained in connection with an attack on Anna Schneider but was released due to insufficient evidence. Andrew Maggio, as we learned earlier, was briefly considered a suspect because a straight razor similar to his was used in the murders. However, he was cleared when his alibi and his report of seeing an unknown man near the scene were verified. Louis Besumer faced indictment for assaulting his mistress, Annie Harriet Lowe, who had accused him of being a German spy, but he was acquitted of all charges. Lewis Oubicon was initially suspected in the Besumer attack but was released because there was no evidence linking him to the crime. An unusual theory proposed that the killer might have had supernatural abilities due to his ability to enter homes undetected, but this idea was soon dismissed. Iorlando and Frank Jordano, competitors of the Cortimiglia family, were suspected of the Cortimiglia murders but were absolved after Rosie Cortimiglia admitted she implicated them out of spite, though some believe she was pressured by the police.

The true identity of the Axeman remains an unsolved mystery, even after more than a century. Colin Wilson, a true crime author, based on accounts by Robert Tallant, proposed that a man named Joseph Mumfre (also spelled Monfre, Momfre or Manfre) might have been the infamous killer. Wilson asserted that Mumfre was reportedly shot to death by the widow of Mike

Pepitone in December 1920 in Los Angeles, California. According to Wilson, Mrs. Pepitone allegedly killed Mumfre in retaliation for her husband's murder. However, the reality was different: Mumfre, who was armed with a pistol, confronted Mrs. Pepitone, demanding $500 and jewelry, and threatened to kill her in the same manner he had her husband. During the altercation, Mrs. Pepitone shot Mumfre at least eleven times, leading to his death; she was subsequently exonerated after it was determined she acted in self-defense.

William A. Kingman of SerialKillerCalendar.com conducted extensive research and uncovered a 1931 newspaper article reporting the arrest of a Joseph Mumphrey in New Orleans for violating the Volstead Act, which banned the production and sale of alcoholic beverages. This raises questions about the claim that Mumfre was killed in Los Angeles in 1920. Michael Newton, another crime writer, had previously found no public records of Joseph Mumfre or Pepitone's widow, but Kingman's findings challenge this, suggesting that Newton's earlier conclusions may have been incomplete. However, Newton's research casts doubt on Wilson's account, which in recent years has come to be regarded as little more than a dramatized legend. Reports from the time suggest that Mumfre was in prison during the Axeman's hiatus between August 1918 and March 1919, and other records indicate he was incarcerated from 1911 through 1918. Nevertheless, records have identified a man named Joseph Mumfre (who last name is, once again, spelled various ways) in New Orleans who was linked to organized crime and implicated in a 1907 bombing, though historical records from that period are inadequate for a definitive identification. The name Momfre also appeared in newspapers in connection with the 1912 shooting of the Schiambra family. Jay Robert Nash suggested that Mumfre could have been a mob hitman extorting Italian grocers, although not all the Axeman's victims fit this profile. Scholar Richard Warner later proposed that Frank "Doc" Mumphrey (1875–1921), who used the alias Monfre or Manfre, might have been the primary suspect. Additionally, some newspaper accounts referred to Mumfre as "Leone J. Manfre," adding another layer of complexity to the case. The various theories share common elements, such as similar surnames, but overall, the evidence remains highly speculative and far from conclusive.

Though his name may be lost to history, the Axeman's legacy lingers. He lives on through stories shared by New Orleanians and has been featured in popular culture, such as major television shows like *American Horror Story: Coven* and novels like Chuck Palahniuk's *Haunted*. And while the terror he inflicted on the city has long since faded, his eerie connection to jazz endures.

Jazz is a part of everyday life for New Orleanians. *Courtesy of Carol M. Highsmith's America, Library of Congress, Prints and Photographs Division.*

To this day, jazz resonates throughout the city. From the moment you step off the plane at Louis Armstrong International Airport, the music greets you. And you hear it again as you venture into the city streets. In New Orleans, jazz is simply everywhere—whether it's drifting out the doors from a live band at iconic venues like Preservation Hall or streaming through the speakers of local shops and cafés. The Axeman need not worry anymore about jazz falling silent. New Orleans will always be a city where the music never stops. It can even be heard emanating from one of the most enigmatic locations in New Orleans: the Haunted Hotel, a place rumored to be the very home of the infamous Axeman himself during his deadly spree and the site of at least ten other unrelated murders.

Now you might be wondering: How could this place allegedly be the Axeman's home when his identity has never been fully uncovered? Well, you're about to find out, and it all begins with Ginger and Bobby Guitreau, two individuals who are the backbone of this historic site.

Ginger (née LeBlanc) grew up in the suburbs near the airport, but she has always considered herself a true New Orleanian at heart. Her childhood was marked by frequent visits to the Garden District, where her family lived and celebrated holidays. When she and Bobby, her junior high sweetheart from Baton Rouge, who is now her husband, decided to pursue work and raise their family in the city, they had no idea their new life would introduce them to a host of spirits.

Ginger and Bobby Guitreau. *Courtesy of Ginger Guitreau.*

Before Hurricane Katrina even made landfall, Bobby was working on Bourbon Street, boarding up buildings in preparation for the storm. Amid the chaos, a stranger approached him, casually dressed in a T-shirt and flip-flops.

"Hey man, could you please help me with boarding up one of my buildings?" the man asked.

Bobby, busy with his work, agreed. "Sure thing. I've got some boards in my truck. Let me just finish getting this board up and I'll help you."

Once Bobby finished the task, the man offered to pay him, holding out a wad of cash. "Here ya go, man. Thank you so much. I couldn't have done this without you!"

Bobby shook his head. "Thanks, but I already had all the boards for the job, so it's not like I spent any money. It was my pleasure to help you out. Keep your money. This is on me."

Reluctantly, the man stuck the money back in his pocket and handed Bobby a card with just a name, Jason, and a phone number—no business details. "At least take this card. Maybe we can connect after the storm."

Bobby took the card and shoved it deep into his pocket but didn't think much of it. "Thanks. I appreciate it." He then provided his number to Jason, just in case.

When Katrina hit, Ginger and Bobby were safe from the storm: they had evacuated to Texas for a little bit. Unfortunately, with so many displaced individuals needing shelter, hotels began turning away evacuees, and their situation grew dire. It was then that Ginger insisted that Bobby call Jason.

"Bobby, you should call him," Ginger urged. "It's worth a shot. He's still in the city. Why don't you at least call him and see how he's doing? Make sure he's okay."

Bobby hesitated. "I don't know, Ginger. I barely know him. We only just met."

Ginger was firm. "Come on, Bobby, it's worth a shot. Can you just try?"

While they were having this discussion, Jason's ear must have been ringing, because suddenly, Bobby's phone began vibrating. "Hey, man! It's Jason. How's everything going?"

Bobby was surprised to hear Jason on the other end of the line and explained their predicament. "Hey Jason, we're not doing so great right now. We're having a tough time finding a place to stay, and we're totally out of money."

Jason's response was unexpectedly reassuring. "Hey man, just drive to Shreveport. I'll take care of everything. If you have a wife and kids, grab them and head this way. Be sure to call me when you get here."

Bobby was skeptical. "Shreveport? Come on, man. There's not a hotel room available anywhere for us right now! Isn't Shreveport plenty crowded with other evacuees?"

Jason's tone was steady. "Just trust me. Get here as soon as you can, and I'll make sure you're taken care of."

True to his word, Jason arranged for them to stay in a house, paid six months' rent in advance and even furnished it. This unexpected kindness provided the stability the Guitreaus needed to rebuild their lives, and they've been working for Jason ever since.

When they finally returned to New Orleans, Jason had acquired several adult clubs on Bourbon Street, which needed renovations. He hired Ginger to clean the clubs and assigned Bobby contract work. It was during this time that Ginger experienced unsettling phenomena for the first time in the French Quarter.

One night, while working alone in one of the clubs, Ginger felt an icy chill and saw a shadowy figure lurking in the dimly lit corner: a cowboy in a long coat and hat who looked as though he stepped straight out of the Wild West. The figure was spooky, disappearing whenever Ginger tried to get a closer look, but she just ignored him, hoping he would leave her alone if she didn't provoke him.

Another unsettling experience came when Ginger was taking photographs at a club on Bourbon Street before its demolition. She took a group photo of the contractors in the building and went home to upload the photos onto her computer. While reviewing the photographs, she was startled to see a familiar yet horrifying figure in one image: the Grim Reaper with a scythe draped over his arms. While the contractors stood smiling off to the side, the eerie figure was front and center, standing ominously in the photo. Ginger was terrified when she saw the figure, not realizing it was an omen of what was to come: her boss, Jason, soon acquired the Haunted Hotel, where Ginger became the property manager and now deals with the paranormal daily.

Ginger started out as a cleaner for the hotel before she was promoted to a managerial position. One evening, after finishing her tasks on the second floor of the main house, Ginger shut off the lights, ensured the area was empty and came downstairs to assist her fellow employee on the first floor. As they worked, both women heard a puzzling sound from above, like a person dragging something too heavy to carry across the hallway. They froze, exchanging bewildered looks, as they were certain no one else was up there.

Along with Ginger's strange encounters, Bobby, while working alone on the property, began experiencing issues of his own. Very often, objects would go missing, a frustrating phenomenon to this day. This happened most often when he was changing or installing locks on doors. He would set the keys down right beneath where he was working, only to find them missing when he went to grab them to make sure they worked. These initial ghostly experiences drove Ginger to look deeper into the history of the hotel.

In 1726, King Louis XV bestowed the tract of land that now contains the Haunted Hotel on the Ursuline nuns. On January 1, 1728, this land transfer was formalized through a deed. Records from 1731 indicate that construction of a house on this property was underway that year, though details about this early structure remain limited.

According to the Vieux Carré Digital Survey, the existing two-story masonry building was originally constructed as a single-story residence around 1825. The structure included two shop windows and two other openings on the ground floor. A detached kitchen from the same period remains on the property. The building was expanded to two stories in the 1880s.

Joseph Guillot acquired the property from the Ursuline nuns on March 8, 1825. Later the same year, on December 20, Edward Lauve purchased the property. On August 5, 1872, Louis Bouzerot acquired it from the Citizens Bank of Louisiana. During this period, the deed described the property as a "large one-story and attic brick dwelling house" with a slate roof and an outhouse. Over time, ownership continued to change, and for most of its history, the buildings on the property were used primarily as family homes. Joseph and Edward still reside on the land in spirit form and have caused quite a hoopla with guests of the Haunted Hotel. Edward tends to lurk in guests' rooms, while Joseph has been known to follow them home. Three separate individuals have reported the same man in period clothing in their home after staying at the hotel.

During a period subsequent to Bouzerot's ownership, it's believed that the property was used as a brothel. While Hotel Villa Convento, just across the street, was known for regularly hosting ladies who were turning tricks, the presence of such individuals at this hotel was much more sporadic. Ms. Marguerite, now one of the hotel's main spirits, is believed to have cared for the property during that time and remains an important figure in its lore. It is said that she allowed the home to be used in this manner to financially support its maintenance. Guests of the hotel today describe an older lady in a dress with a high collar, an apron and a bonnet frequently seen looking out the upstairs window of the main house.

After Ginger learned about the origins of the property and told Bobby about them, the couple was eager to explore the premises. Their trip to the attic was meant to be a simple exploration, but it quickly turned into something far more intriguing. The attic itself was unremarkable, a typical dusty space with the usual signs of age and disuse. However, the moment Bobby laid eyes on the gleaming floorboards, their potential immediately became clear. These floorboards, cut from a rare and ancient cypress tree, were in exceptional condition—too valuable to be left in the attic to rot.

When the decision was made to repurpose them for the hotel, Bobby carefully began prying up the boards. As he worked, he was already envisioning the doors they would make, unique pieces that would elevate the entire property. An employee from a nearby company had noticed the quality of the wood and offered Bobby a small sum for it, but Bobby had bigger plans. He knew these floorboards could be worth much more if reused creatively. And he was right: after the work was complete, those doors were appraised at $15,000 to $25,000 each.

But as Bobby pulled back the last few floorboards, he discovered something neither he nor Ginger could have anticipated. Beneath the planks, nestled in the shadows, was an old axe. Its sharp metal blade was stained a deep garnet hue, leaving a trace of whatever had transpired.

It was easy to rationalize. Perhaps the axe had been used to slaughter animals for food, especially in the days when the property housed families. But why was it hidden away so carefully beneath the floorboards? And furthermore, who did the blood belong to?

Neither the Mumfre surname nor any name resembling it appears on the official deed of the property. Nonetheless, it's entirely conceivable that the Axeman could have lived at this address. After all, property records are missing, and there's always the possibility that someone associated with the property, unaware of his nefarious acts, might have allowed him to stay on-

Bobby Guitreau discovered this axe beneath the floorboards of the attic on the property where the Haunted Hotel now stands at 623 Ursulines Avenue. *Courtesy of Amy Shabluk.*

site. And in a strange twist, what if someone who was listed on the deed was actually the killer all along? Just some food for thought!

This location seems chock-full of things that have yet to be discovered. Lest you think it couldn't get any weirder than finding a bloodied axe, the Guitreaus discovered a handful of other artifacts beneath the flooring. Among the most notable in addition to the axe were a charcoal drawing of a little boy from the 1800s that was tucked behind a framed page of a magazine and a peculiar hand-carved wooden mirror that seemed to tell a story of its own. At first, Bobby believed it to be a black-and-white portrait in an intricate wooden frame. The image was of an elderly woman in a long dress, with a somber and downtrodden expression, her eyes fixated downward. However, as Bobby brushed off the "portrait" to get a clearer look, he realized it was not a portrait at all but the glass of a mirror. Wiping off the dust, he saw his own reflection staring back at him. The detailed image in the dust was deeply unsettling to Bobby. The mirror now hangs in the hotel lobby, along with the other artifacts. Those who encounter it are overcome by feelings of revulsion.

Once the axe was uncovered, it became clear that the Axeman's spirit was alive and well.

Misti Gaither, a renowned psychic medium and host of the talk show *Quest: A Journey Into True Crime and the Paranormal*, works alongside her wife,

Catherine, as a prominent member of the Louisiana Spirits investigative team and is the current resident paranormal investigator at the Haunted Hotel. One evening, she was conducting a paranormal investigation with her best friend, psychic medium Cari Roy, in two of the most haunted rooms inside the main house, Room 113 and Room 114. Starting in Room 114, Misti began using dowsing rods, and both women asked questions of the spirits. After asking if one of the spirits had lived during the 1900s, the rods crossed, and Misti was almost immediately overwhelmed with feelings of intense anger. Cari sensed a palpable energy shift, noticing that Misti was no longer her usual fun, happy-go-lucky self.

A wave of frigid air encircled Misti and Cari as the temperature in Room 114 plummeted to sixty-two degrees. The atmosphere grew heavy, and the biting cold left them shivering uncontrollably. Finding the intensity overwhelming, they decided to move to another room. As they entered Room 113, the cold was even more pronounced; they estimated the temperature was around fifty-two degrees.

Following this, Misti and Cari proceeded to investigate the Axeman's Room, Room B6, the very room where he is believed to have once stayed. This room, located at the far right end of the second story in a yellow motel-style building, was originally part of the former slave quarters.

Bobby, an employee of the property (not to be confused with Bobby Guitreau, Ginger's husband), shared his chilling experience on the one-hundred-year anniversary of the day the Axeman wrote his infamous letter. He recounted the story with an uneasy chuckle, saying:

> *It was the middle of the night, and I was fixing up a room for a couple from the UK. There were a few flies in the bathroom, and I killed them. But then, around two o'clock in the morning, I get a knock on my door. The couple told me there were bugs in their room. So I offered to switch them to a different room, and they agreed. They asked if I wanted to come up and see the bugs first. When I got up there, I couldn't believe it—there were about three hundred flies all over the bathroom walls and ceiling. The next morning, we called an exterminator. As soon as he saw the flies, he said, "I know exactly what this is. These flies only swarm around dead carcasses. You probably have something dead in the attic." He went up to check the attic and came back down completely flabbergasted. He found maggots and larvae covering the beams and HVAC vents from the center of the room all the way to the bathroom—right where the original Axeman supposedly stayed. He didn't know that at the time.*

A bird's-eye view of the courtyard and motel-style building at the Haunted Hotel. *Courtesy of Herb Leonard Jr. of Phototype Productions.*

During Cari and Misti's investigation in that very room, Cari began hearing the letter *R* in her head. Psychics often hear things phonetically, so she told Misti she was getting the letter *R* for the real name of the Axeman. Misti, being a medium herself, had written down a name earlier in the day without telling Cari and kept it in her pocket. During the investigation, she reached into her pocket and pulled out the piece of paper, which said, "Robert." This was all captured on camera as they were filming the investigation.

Cari began getting the feeling that something sinister was lurking down in the courtyard. Many psychics have detected a similar presence in that area. In Ginger's experience, the entity of the Axeman often meanders around the garden, and he mostly behaves himself, so long as the jazz keeps flowing. One psychic, however, told Ginger that there were two souls buried on-site, one of them a person so vile that their coffin was encased in lead to entrap their spirit and keep it from escaping. Who could possibly have a more malevolent spirit than the Axeman?

Cheyanne Disé, a highly regarded evidential medium and psychic previously based in New Orleans, has had a distinguished career exploring the supernatural. Her journey began in 1977 when her childhood home was plagued by intense poltergeist activity witnessed by her entire family. This early exposure ignited her passion for the paranormal. After moving out of her childhood home in 1987, she experienced a period of quiet until 1994, when she relocated to San Jose, California. There, she and her friends encountered numerous unexplained phenomena, including full apparitions and doors that moved on their own. These experiences led her to formally study mediumship in 1988. By 2003, Cheyanne was actively working as a medium and psychic, hosting a public access paranormal show in Seattle, Washington, and leading ghost tours at Pike Place Market and Butterworth Mortuary. Her move to New Orleans in 2019 marked a new chapter in her career, in which she continued to explore the supernatural while also working as an artist and spiritual mentor.

In July 2024, Cheyanne was invited to a three-day lockdown event at the Haunted Hotel, where she had an extremely active night. On the first night, after dinner and under the light of the full Buck Moon, Cheyanne chose to investigate the Axeman's Room alone, carrying a custom pendulum gifted to her earlier.

Cheyanne approached the investigation with an open mind, aiming to establish a connection with any spirit rather than focusing solely on the Axeman. Settling on the bed, Cheyanne engaged in breathing exercises to attune herself to the room's energy. After about ten to fifteen minutes, she began using the pendulum to verify her intuitive impressions.

During her session, Cheyanne noticed a figure moving past the window in the door. Assuming it was other ghost hunters, she went to check but found only a couple sitting at the opposite end of the courtyard, in front of the industrial fan. Returning to her session, she resumed using the pendulum and inquired if the spirit's name was Paula. The pendulum confirmed this. She then asked if Paula had been alive in the 1980s, but the answer was no; Paula had lived in the 1920s.

As Cheyanne continued, she saw a vision of a wounded wrist and hand. She asked if Paula had experienced a fall, and the pendulum responded affirmatively. The air around her grew thick with the strong smell of cinnamon, and she felt gentle tugs on her hair, signs of the spirit's presence. After some time, a sense of calm settled over her, and she expressed her gratitude for the connection.

Leaving the room, Cheyanne joined the couple she had seen earlier. The man turned out to be Jereme Leonard, known as the Cajun Demonologist, from Netflix's *28 Days Haunted*. As they spoke, Cheyanne shared her experience in the Axeman's Room. Jereme revealed that he had witnessed a vision mirroring Cheyanne's description: Paula's jump from the rooftop and the resulting injury to her arm, which included a contorted bone from the fall. Cheyanne believes the shadow that passed her room was the apparition of Paula in her final moments before her life came to an end.

On the second night, Cheyanne led a séance on the main building's upper floor with two small groups. The séance was revealing: one participant reported a smell of cinnamon, validating Cheyanne's earlier experience with Paula. The spirit of a man named Phillip came through this time, claiming to know of a butcher from the 700 block of Ursulines. In another session, the spirit of a lady named Rose made her presence known, recounting a tragic fall down a steep spiral staircase, though it did not result in death. During this same session, it was also disclosed that a former employee of the property ended her life in 1992. Cheyanne came to believe that the property was a vortex to the other side, estimating there to be more than twenty-seven spirits in total.

In addition to Cheyanne, other mediums have picked up the energy of a domineering man who was abusive to his young daughter. Both father and daughter are thought to still be on the property. The main building houses the nameless little girl's spirit. She tends to avoid interaction, her voice often drowned out by her father's authoritative presence. Two individuals who continually attempted to communicate with the little girl despite her lack of response found their bodies covered in scratch marks.

Another couple, the wife eager to stay at the hotel and the husband reluctant, faced an unexpected ordeal in their assigned room. The husband, who was already very leery of staying in a place called the Haunted Hotel, experienced primal fear when he was yanked out of bed by his ankle in the night like a child playing hooky from school. The man was in a full-blown panic, and a high-pitched shriek escaped his lips in the darkness. His wife, unable to see him clearly, found his fear amusing and laughed uncontrollably. "Oh my God, you just screamed like a little girl!" she exclaimed, her laughter echoing through the room. It was undeniable that the husband was not amused in the least.

The next morning, Ginger approached the couple. "I hope you had a restful stay," she said with a friendly smile.

The husband returned her kind comment with a filthy look.

"Oh no," Ginger said. "What happened? Is everything alright?"

"Ask her," the man replied tersely, gesturing toward his wife.

His wife, still amused, shared the story with Ginger. This most certainly was the last night the couple would ever spend at the Haunted Hotel.

Herb Leonard Jr., a former assistant property manager at the Haunted Hotel, worked there just before Mardi Gras in 2021, taking on various roles, such as groundskeeper, front desk worker and housekeeper. He had been with the company for nearly eleven years, working intermittently at various properties in different roles. A position opened up at the Haunted Hotel on his return from Los Angeles, California, where he had relocated after his house flooded during Hurricane Ida.

In addition to his role at the hotel, Herb is a full-time freelance photographer and art dealer through his business, Phototype Productions. During his time at the Haunted Hotel, he was designated its official photographer, capturing the property's unique character and historical essence.

Herb had a memorable paranormal experience while staying at the hotel. One evening, as he settled into his room, he was sitting on the floor, listening to music, when he suddenly felt a gentle push on his back. The sensation was as if something had nudged him lightly to get his attention. Despite looking around and checking under the bed, he couldn't find any cause for the sensation. Afterward, he laughed to himself, acknowledging the unusual feeling with a lighthearted comment: "Yep, this place is haunted."

A week later, a Spanish dancer who frequently stayed at the hotel mentioned hearing about ghostly children playing around. She suggested that the soft push Herb experienced might have been from one of these spirits. A few months later, the hotel placed a book in the lobby for guests to record their ghostly encounters or thoughts about the property. While some guests dismissed the hauntings, many others shared stories that seemed to support the hotel's haunted reputation. This was further substantiated when two separate individuals, who did not know each other and had no prior knowledge of the hotel's history, reported having the same exact dream about two little boys trying to get into their rooms at night.

Herb made a point of maintaining the property with respect and care, honoring its history and ensuring it was well-preserved. He was committed to keeping the space in outstanding condition, as if its former residents were still living there. After all, he reasoned, no one wants their home mistreated by visitors.

Reflecting on the local belief in hauntings, Herb said, "It's New Orleans—almost every place is haunted, even ya grandma house. And if you're from here, you've had at least three experiences without even trying."

If I had to choose the most likely place in the city to encounter a ghost, the Haunted Hotel would be it. Ginger's dedication to the hotel is evident in every detail, from the "bloody" water fountain in the courtyard (which is actually dyed with red food coloring) to the stand-up cards in each room that read, "This room was professionally cleaned. Hope you don't get murdered

Spooky little touches in every room make one's stay at the Haunted Hotel an unforgettable experience. *Author photo.*

in your sleep. Love, the Axeman." Ginger even plants small glow-in-the-dark ghosts in every room, aiming to give all guests a ghost sighting, as real spirits don't always show up on cue. The Haunted Hotel truly lives up to its name, with genuine hauntings that make it the ultimate destination for any paranormal enthusiast. While fear might be just a night away, it's all part of what makes this hotel such a thrill.

CHAPTER 9

JACKSON SCARE

PLACE D'ARMES HOTEL
625 ST. ANN STREET
NEW ORLEANS, LOUISIANA 70116

The Place d'Armes Hotel, the most centrally located hotel in the French Quarter and only hotel in Jackson Square, derives its name from the historic square originally known as Place d'Armes. The square, established in 1721 by LeBlond de la Tour, a French military architect and the engineer-in-chief of Louisiana, along with his assistant, Adrien de Pauger, served as a major hub for the colony. Soldiers most often assembled there for musterings and military ceremonies. The square functioned as a key gathering spot for New Orleans' colonial French residents, who came together there for church services, to welcome incoming ships and for public celebrations or executions. Major General Andrew Jackson reviewed local troops there in December 1814, a pivotal moment in the War of 1812. In 1851, following the erection of a statue honoring General Jackson for his leadership in the Battle of New Orleans, the square was renamed Jackson Square.

Most of the land surrounding Jackson Square was eventually allocated to employees and investors of the Compagnie des Indes, a trading company authorized by King Louis XV. This company was managed by John Law, a Scottish financier who gained favor with French regent Philippe II, Duke of Orléans. As a result, the company granted parcels of land to early settlers in the French colonies, who then built their homes there.

Like many hotels in the city, this one consists of multiple parcels. The history of 623–625 St. Ann Street, the building that now serves as the hotel's lobby, closely mirrors that of its neighboring property at 617–619

Pictured is the St. Louis Cathedral, the most iconic landmark in Jackson Square. *Author photo.*

St. Ann Street. The land, which initially comprised a larger side street lot of 50 by 150 feet, was given by the Compagnie des Indes to Sieur Richaume on January 1, 1722. Sieur Richaume soon transferred the lot to Augustin Langlois, who'd sold it to Father Raphael de Luxembourg by 1725. Father

Raphael de Luxembourg, rector of St. Louis Parish Church, which would later become the St. Louis Cathedral, founded the Capuchin School on this site. The Place d'Armes Hotel would later be established on the former site of this educational institution. A modest one-room building served as the school, offering instruction in reading, writing, music, French, Latin and religion for beginners, as well as liberal arts for more advanced students. Early teachers included Pierre Fleurtet, a layman, and Capuchin Brothers St. Julien and Cyril. By 1740, both the school and the surrounding fence had deteriorated beyond repair, leading to the school's closure. Today, a historical marker on the side of the building on St. Ann Street commemorates this significant educational landmark.

After the school closed, the property became part of Jean-Baptiste Destrehan's grand estate, which stretched from this site to the corner of St. Ann and Chartres Streets, encompassing additional land along Chartres Street. The estate featured a magnificent French Colonial house with a sturdy brick ground floor and an upper level constructed of *colombage*. In addition to the main residence, the estate included servant quarters, a kitchen and a coach house. This expansive and beautifully maintained property was surrounded by lush gardens, where vibrant greenery flourished in the abundant sunshine and humidity. Destrehan's home showcased his immense wealth and prominence, reflecting his status as treasurer of the Royal Navy and a leading figure in colonial New Orleans.

Upon Destrehan's death on February 26, 1765, the property passed to Pierre Philippe de Marigny. The large colonial home on this prominent corner lot was burned down in the 1788 fire that devastated much of the city. By that time, the property had been subdivided, and from then on, this specific lot existed as a separate entity. After the fire, a basic wooden warehouse was constructed on the site. Marcus Tio purchased the property in 1795 and retained ownership for twenty-seven years. When he died in 1822, the estate passed to his nephew, Francisco Tio, who lived there until 1856 and is believed to have made significant changes to the property. During the end of his tenure, it was listed as a two-and-a-half-story brick townhouse with a side carriageway.

Dating the current building is difficult due to the extensive restorations that have altered much of its original character. While it's possible that Marcus Tio built the earlier structure, the changes made during subsequent restorations, particularly in the twentieth century, stripped the building of much of its authentic historical detail. The property also included two-story outbuildings at the rear, which were once used as a woodworking shop and, later, as a wine warehouse. By 1964, the entire courtyard had been filled in, and the buildings had been modernized and converted into apartments.

The lot changed hands several times before being acquired by Angelo Glorioso on January 27, 1914. Glorioso, an immigrant from Sicily, utilized the property as both a family home and a grocery warehouse. Glorioso bequeathed the property to his only daughter, Mary Ann Glorioso Valentino, who inherited it on June 26, 1951.

In November 1963, the *Times-Picayune* reported that the New Orleans Board of Zoning Adjustments was considering a proposal to convert the apartment complex into a fifty-unit motel. This proposal marked the beginning of a significant redevelopment.

In 1964, the property underwent a major transformation: the construction of a new five-story building, the Place d'Armes Motor Hotel, which replaced the previous wine storage warehouse. The hotel was eventually renamed and is now known simply as the Place d'Armes Hotel. Today it is still operated by the Valentino family, and they own and operate several other properties as well, including the Alder Hotel, the Brakeman Hotel, the Basin Street Hotel, the Hotel St. Marie, the French Market Inn and the Prince Conti Hotel. The Place d'Armes remains their most historic property. The hotel is made up of a total of seven buildings, including five constructed in the 1800s and two added in the 1960s, as earlier structures from the settlement era were lost to the city's major conflagrations.

The Place d'Armes Hotel is ideally situated, just a short walk from Café du Monde, where you can savor a café au lait and delicious beignets. Enjoy a memorable jazz brunch at the neighboring Muriel's restaurant (which is super haunted) and visit their ghost table and Séance Lounge to learn more about their ghostly lore. For a more eccentric dining experience, the New Orleans Vampire Café is just a few steps away and even serves wine in blood bags. Surrounded by vibrant streets filled with nightlife and entertainment, the hotel is perfect for those eager to experience the city's energetic atmosphere. With a variety of shops, restaurants and attractions nearby, there's plenty to see and do. However, while the Place d'Armes Hotel offers an unbeatable location, guests who stay on-site should prepare for a haunting experience. If anyone knows this for a fact, it's Brenda Gale Butler.

Brenda has been a devoted visitor to New Orleans for years. Although she resides in Missouri, her soft spot for the city has led her to return repeatedly, always enchanted by its lively spirit. During one of her visits, she chose to stay at the Place d'Armes Hotel, intrigued by its proximity to Jackson Square

A quiet moment along the sidewalk outside the Place d'Armes Hotel. *Courtesy of Amy Shabluk.*

and the stories of hauntings associated with the property. Brenda hoped for a thrilling yet pleasant paranormal experience, but she did not anticipate encountering something malevolent.

During her initial stay at the Place d'Armes Hotel, Brenda did not have any personal experiences with the supernatural. While waiting in the lobby for an Uber, she overheard a conversation between other guests and the desk clerk. The guests were complaining about noisy children in the rooms above them the previous night. The clerk replied that there were no children—or any guests—in those rooms and noted that reports of noisy youngsters were a frequent occurrence.

On her next trip to New Orleans, Brenda stayed in Room 218. The first night, she felt great and was delighted to be in her favorite city, savoring the views of Jackson Square from her balcony. However, as soon as she entered the room and settled into bed, she sensed an unsettling presence that seemed to object to her stay. Suddenly, she was overcome by a severe illness, and as the minutes ticked by, her condition only worsened. After suffering in complete misery for over an hour, barely able to move, she pleaded aloud, "Please stop!" Almost immediately, her condition improved, and she went from being deathly ill to completely fine. The next night, this same scenario happened again at the exact same time. This time, she said, "I know who you are, and I respect your space. Please stop, and I'll be gone by tomorrow." Instantly, Brenda felt like her normal self again, with no symptoms whatsoever. The experience was so frightening that she asked the bellhop to retrieve her luggage the next morning, as she refused to enter that room ever again. Brenda cautions others against staying in the same room due to the wicked entity that calls it home.

In addition to the vicious entity and the noisy children's spirits, there have been numerous other supernatural happenings at the Place d'Armes Hotel. One particularly striking encounter involved guests with balcony rooms overlooking the Magnolia Courtyard who observed a soldier on horseback. Initially, they were mesmerized to see such a sight at the hotel, thinking it was part of a ceremonial event. However, their astonishment turned to disbelief as the soldier and his horse suddenly leapt into the side of the building and vanished, leaving everyone stunned and questioning the reality of what they had witnessed.

One of the housekeepers who happened to be in the courtyard during this incident witnessed the spectacle. She was profoundly affected by the experience, describing it as "mind-bending." She felt as if she were trapped in a dream, struggling to reconcile the event with reality. It was a moment

The Magnolia Courtyard is known for its frequent ghost sightings. *Courtesy of Amy Shabluk.*

that defied explanation and left her grappling with the intensity of what she had seen.

Moreover, another guest was sitting on her balcony when she noticed a man on the one next to hers, whom she presumed to be another guest. She struck up a conversation with him, and they shared stories and laughter, creating an immediate friendship. Later, buzzing with excitement, she shared her encounter with the front desk agent, only to be met with disbelief.

"Ma'am, there's no one staying in that room," the agent replied.

When the guest described the man, a bearded figure who exuded a genuine warmth, the front desk agent's eyes widened. "Oh, him! That's our ghost!" she exclaimed lightheartedly.

Based on phenomena reported by both staff and guests, many believe this spirit to be the first headmaster of the Capuchin school that once occupied the site.

While much of the paranormal activity at the hotel is somatic and visual in nature, there are also auditory occurrences. Guests who stay in Room 508 struggle to fall asleep, kept awake by persistent whispers that seem to come out of nowhere. Others have reported hearing the eerie strains of Gregorian chants, prayers and other religious sounds drifting through the halls. A TripAdvisor user, staceydaze, from Boston, Massachusetts, started a TripAdvisor forum asking others if they had any paranormal experiences at the Place d'Armes Hotel—and many users chimed in, sharing a variety of eerie encounters.

Curious August, who hails from Oakland, California, checked into Room 216 for a two-night stay in 2010. On the first afternoon and once again in the evening, at approximately ten o'clock, they were captivated by the sound of Gregorian chanting filling their room. They stepped out onto the balcony, hoping to trace the melody to its source, but were met with silence outside.

Puzzled, Curious approached the porter and inquired if there was a church service happening nearby that might be responsible for the chanting. The porter listened to their description with a knowing smile and mentioned that while guests in that room often reported hearing soft clapping and chanting, what Curious had experienced was notably different and more resonant.

The main cathedral, just a block and a half away, was not hosting any services that night. The next evening, Curious's friend also heard the mysterious chant. Though unaware of any haunting rumors associated with the Place d'Armes Hotel, Curious found the experience to be a hauntingly beautiful and memorable highlight of their stay.

As frequently as the sound of chanting drifts through the hotel, the presence of female spirits manifests. Surprisingly, most of the apparitions on the property are those of women, contrasting with the hotel's history, which might suggest a predominance of male spirits.

One of the most frequently witnessed spirits at the Place d'Armes Hotel is a dignified woman of African descent. She is often seen wearing a long, flowing gown with her head wrapped in a tignon. Poised and serene, she stands in the Magnolia Courtyard, quietly observing the surroundings. Guests who have rooms overlooking this courtyard sometimes report seeing her standing there. When they look away briefly and then return their gaze, she mysteriously disappears.

Two other individuals also shared paranormal encounters on the TripAdvisor forum from stays in 2010, each pertaining to different female entities that they saw. Bunnie, from Palm Harbor, Florida, shared a personal experience from her stay at the hotel. In her account, she described encountering a different apparition than the one frequently seen in the courtyard. She and her husband had stayed at the hotel many times, always hoping for a "haunting," and during their visit in 2010, they finally got their wish.

On checking in, they each received a key at the front desk, but when they arrived at their room (possibly Room 301), they found that neither key worked. As they made their way back to the front desk, they encountered a woman standing next to a laundry cart around the corner from their room. The woman asked if they were having trouble with their key. When they confirmed, she handed them a new key, mentioning that this sort of thing happened a lot and that the new key would work. To their relief, it did.

Bunnie found it strange that the woman hadn't asked for their room number, but since the key was already marked with the correct room number, they didn't think much more of it. After placing their belongings in the room, they left to walk around the French Quarter.

On their way out, they stopped at the front desk to return the two keys that didn't work and mentioned that they had one that did. The man at the desk, looking puzzled, asked, "Where did you get this key?"

Bunnie told him about the maid who had given them the key. To her surprise, the clerk responded, "The maids left a few hours ago."

Although unsettled by the strange encounter, the couple received a second working key and continued their evening, watching a parade and having dinner before heading back to the hotel to sleep.

Later that night, however, they were awakened by something much more chilling. In the middle of the night, Bunnie saw a young woman standing in their room, dressed in Victorian-era clothing: a heavy coat and a bonnet, with long, light brown hair flowing beneath it. Startled and confused, Bunnie yelled at the woman, waking her husband in the process. As soon as she did, the woman vanished. Despite the invasive encounter, Bunnie and her husband were undeterred and planned to return to the hotel the following weekend, eager for another chance to see a ghost.

Another individual from Daphne, Alabama, who went by the username Fyre, recounted another mysterious woman on the property. They were in New Orleans for their wedding and were invited upstairs by one of their husband's relatives, who was staying at the hotel. As they explored the upper floors, they realized they had taken a wrong turn and needed to retrace their steps.

At the opposite end of the hallway, they saw a woman dressed in a long gown and a large hat. Although it's not unusual for people in New Orleans to dress up, the sight of her still stood out. However, when Fyre reached the end of the hall where the woman had been, she was nowhere to be found. There were no signs of an exit or a door she could have used to leave, and Fyre would have heard a door closing if she had entered a room.

The woman was neither frightening nor transparent, and Fyre described her dress as either a light pink or cream color. Her sudden disappearance without a trace left Fyre puzzled, unable to explain the mysterious vanishing of the well-dressed woman.

The Place d'Armes Hotel is more than just a place to stay; it's a gateway to the past. Its haunted halls are filled with the echoes of lives lived and lost. As you wander through its corridors, are you willing to listen? The choice is yours. But be warned, the spirits that reside within these walls may not all be as friendly as they seem. Step across the threshold at your own risk.

CHAPTER 10

THE GHOSTLY GRIP

HOTEL ST. PIERRE
911 BURGUNDY STREET
NEW ORLEANS, LOUISIANA 70116

Hotel St. Pierre is a unique collection of French Colonial and Creole cottages and six distinct courtyards, each with its own character, coming together to create a single hotel. Among the notable buildings are the Peyroux House and the Jazz Cottage, both rich in history and said to be home to restless spirits. As we explore these two significant structures, we will uncover the spirited encounters that have turned this hotel into a popular destination for paranormal enthusiasts.

In 1754, François Caue acquired the entire block that would later become home to one of the oldest residences in New Orleans. His daughter, Mary Susanna, married Gabriel Peyroux de la Roche Molive, a Frenchman from Mortaine known for his impulsive nature. In 1777, Gabriel purchased a plantation on Bayou Road, where the house originally stood. Not long after relocating, he commissioned a new house to be built before the previous one was even completed. The original structure was then moved and reassembled at its current location, 911 Burgundy Street, on the corner of Burgundy and Dumaine, thanks to the skilled craftsmanship of builder Maurice Milon. Milon constructed the residence in the traditional "briquette-entre-poteaux" style, using bricks set between wooden posts. The walls were made from a blend of Mississippi River mud, Spanish moss and horsehair, showcasing the resourcefulness of the region. This remarkable structure not only served as the Peyroux family home until 1850, surviving the city's devastating fires, but also adapted to the evolving needs of the community, becoming an

The Peyroux House. *Courtesy of Amy Shabluk.*

apothecary, a collection of apartments, a small warehouse and a department store over the years.

In 1961, the adjacent yellow building at 1017 Dumaine Street, now the hotel's lobby, gained fame as the world's first jazz museum. This vibrant space became a treasure trove of jazz history, housing an impressive collection of memorabilia, including Louis Armstrong's trumpet and the groundbreaking recordings of Kid Ory, Jelly Roll Morton and Cozy Cole. The building was also a prominent venue for jazz funerals and a starting point for many second lines.

In November 1969, the Crossbeam Motel opened on the property and boasted iron grille gates in the newspaper. Over the years, it has continued to host visitors, including notable names like jazz legend Louis Armstrong and American playwright and screenwriter Tennessee Williams, who penned the famous *A Streetcar Named Desire*. Despite its history not being as elaborate as those of other locations, there's an unsettling undercurrent here that cannot be ignored.

At Hotel St. Pierre, ghostly encounters are as common as a housekeeper changing the bedsheets. One of the most frequently reported experiences is the sound of loud footsteps that disrupt guests' sleep. Another occurrence is the sight of a spectral figure outside the main entrance: a man appearing to be pushing fifty, clad in a color-coordinated blue shirt and trousers, finished off with polished black leather boots that gleam in the light. This ghost is believed to be associated with the role of carriage master for the

A historic photo, believed to have been taken in the 1950s, of the building now known as the Jazz Cottage. *Courtesy of Richard Koch Papers and Photographs, Southeastern Architectural Archive, Tulane University Special Collections, Tulane University Libraries.*

Peyroux family; many believe he is still waiting for the family to come home once more.

The hotel's haunted reputation is further reinforced by a hair-raising account on TripAdvisor from a guest named Annie G., a self-proclaimed atheist. On her first night, she was awakened by her daughter's voice urging her to wake up. She reached for her cell phone to illuminate the room, and the light revealed a figure sitting at the foot of her bed, facing away from her, its head draped in a blanket like a headscarf. Panicked, she leapt from the bed and turned on the light, only to find her room empty and her daughter safe in a separate room. This eerie encounter left Annie questioning her lack of belief in an afterlife.

Yet something far more sinister lurks in these guest rooms: a clammy hand that snatches at unsuspecting souls. These chilling encounters often happen when a guest drops an item, perhaps their phone, AirPods or charging cord. As they lean down to retrieve it, they're abruptly gripped by the icy touch of a ghostly hand seizing theirs with unyielding force. But it doesn't end there. Sometimes, the damp spectral hand snakes up from the foot of the bed, sliding beneath the covers before clamping onto the guest's legs in the dead of night and violently yanking them to the floor. One female guest awakened in sheer terror to find the same clammy hand pressed firmly over her mouth, as if it were intent on smothering her. She was paralyzed by dread and unable to let out an audible scream, her heart racing as she struggled to push away the unseen menace. When she finally managed to free herself from the entity's grip, her breath came in heavy gasps and her heart raced in her chest as she realized she was utterly alone. No trace of the being that had just tried to silence her forever remained.

These encounters have left many guests terrified, and the strange, ghostly grip has become the defining mark of the hauntings here, enough to send chills through anyone who experiences it. No room on this property carries the title of "most haunted"—as any room could be the one where you feel the cold grip of an unseen presence.

BIBLIOGRAPHY

Acadiana Profile. "If Walls Could Talk." November 7, 2017. https://acadianaprofile.com.

Al-Hatlani, Alana. "New Orleans's Legendary Carousel Bar Is Turning 75." *Southern Living*, September 10, 2024.

Andrew Jackson Hotel. https://www.andrewjacksonhotel.com.

Andrews, Stefan. "The Original Song 'The House of the Rising Sun' Is Older Than New Orleans." The Vintage News, January 21, 2017. https://www.thevintagenews.com.

Asher, Sally. "Last Days of Storyville." My New Orleans, September 29, 2017. https://www.myneworleans.com.

Audubon Cottages. "The Story Behind the Historic Cottages: John James Audubon." Audubon Cottages, 2024. https://www.auduboncottages.com.

Barclay, Shelly. "The Zach and Addie Murder/Suicide." Historic Mysteries, March 11, 2014. https://www.historicmysteries.com.

Bartlette, DeLani R. "The Gruesome Tale of Zack Bowen and Addie Hall—and What It Says About Our Fascination with True Crime." Medium, April 29, 2019. https://delanirbartlette.medium.com.

Beauchamp, Nicole. *Haunted Bay City, Michigan.* The History Press, 2020.

Beck Technology. "Story Behind the Building: The House of the Rising Sun." 2024. https://www.beck-technology.com.

Belsom, Jack. "A History of Opera in New Orleans." New Orleans Opera Association, 2023. https://neworleansopera.org.

Benson, Jyl. "Sightseeing in the 'Old Square.'" FrenchQuarter.com, 2017. https://www.frenchquarter.com.

Bentley, Charlotte Alice. "Resituating Transatlantic Opera: The Case of the Théâtre d'Orléans, New Orleans, 1819–1859." Apollo: University of Cambridge Repository. https://doi.org/10.17863/CAM.21187.

Beviglia, Jim. "Behind the Song Lyrics: 'House of the Rising Sun,' the Animals." *American Songwriter*, March 14, 2022. https://americansongwriter.com.

Bourbon Orleans Hotel. "Our History." March 16, 2022. https://www.bourbonorleans.com.

Branley, Edward (NOLA History Guy). "Locoul Family Tomb, New Orleans, Orleans Parish, Louisiana." October 21, 2018. https://nolahistoryguy.com.

BuzzFeed Unsolved Network. "The Haunted Quarters of the Dauphine Orleans Hotel." YouTube, June 2, 2017. https://youtu.be/thR7IhHV554.

Campanella, Richard. "Before Storyville: Vice Districts in Antebellum New Orleans, Part II: Gallatin Street." *Preservation in Print* (Preservation Research Center), October 2015. https://richcampanella.com.

———. "'A Scene of Tumultuous Confusion': The History of Slave Auctioning at Hewlett's Exchange." Preservation Resource Center of New Orleans, August 1, 2023. https://prcno.org.

———. "The St. Louis and the St. Charles: New Orleans Legacy of Showcase Exchange Hotels." *Preservation in Print* (Preservation Research Center), April 2015. https://richcampanella.com.

Carrasco, Isabel. "What's the Deal with the Real House of the Rising Sun?" Cultura Colectiva, January 21, 2020. https://culturacolectiva.com.

Clark, Emily. *Voices from an Early American Convent.* LSU Press, 2009.

Collins C. Diboll Vieux Carré Survey. "409–419 Dauphine St." Historic New Orleans Collection. https://www.hnoc.org.

———. "919–923 Royal St." Historic New Orleans Collection. https://www.hnoc.org.

———. "616 Ursulines St." Historic New Orleans Collection. https://www.hnoc.org.

———. "Storyville: Madams & Music." Historic New Orleans Collection. https://www.hnoc.org.

Cultural Landscape Foundation. "Old Ursuline Convent." 2024. https://www.tclf.org.

Daily Picayune (New Orleans, LA). "Louisiana Story in Little Chapters: The Jesuits Early Settlers—Great Fires—First French Colony." October 26, 1986.

Danner, Jim (Guest Services/Front Office at Olivier House Hotel.) Response to "What a Fantastic Place to Stay!" Review of Olivier House Hotel, TripAdvisor, April 15, 2021. https://www.tripadvisor.com.

Dauphine Orleans Hotel. https://www.dauphineorleans.com.

Davis, Miriam. "The Axeman of New Orleans Preyed on Italian Immigrants." *Smithsonian Magazine*, February 15, 2018. https://www.smithsonianmag.com.

Days, Stacy. "Any Haunted Place D'Armes Stories?" TripAdvisor New Orleans Travel Forum, 2010. https://www.tripadvisor.com.

Dinstel, Donna, and James Bianco. "Arnaud Magnon (1741–1821)." Find a Grave, February 3, 2016. https://www.findagrave.com.

———. "Elizabeth Louise 'Lize' Forstall Poeyfarre." Find a Grave, February 3, 2016. https://www.findagrave.com.

———. "Jean Baptiste Poeyfarre (Unknown–1824)." Find a Grave, February 3, 2016. https://www.findagrave.com.

Donnella, Leah. "How Yellow Fever Turned New Orleans into the 'City of the Dead.'" NPR, October 31, 2018. https://www.npr.org.

Dunnell, Tony. "Carousel Bar." Atlas Obscura, August 13, 2010. https://www.atlasobscura.com.

Duplechien. "Olivier House Hotel, New Orleans, Louisiana." *Haunted Nation* (blog), September 29, 2016. https://hauntednation.blogspot.com.

E., Michelle. "Delightful and Quaint Hotel in the Heart of the French Quarter." Review of Olivier House Hotel, TripAdvisor, February 2018. https://www.tripadvisor.com.

Editors of Encyclopedia Britannica. "Louisiana Purchase." Britannica. https://www.britannica.com.

———. "Volstead Act: United States [1919]." Edited by Jeff Wallenfeldt. Britannica, August 11, 2016. https://www.britannica.com.

Fox, F.G. *Bizarre New Orleans.* St. Expedite Press, 1997.

G., Annie. "Haunted. Bring a Friend." Review of Hotel St. Pierre, TripAdvisor, August 2018. https://www.tripadvisor.com.

Galaxy Music Notes. "The Story of Folk and Rock Song 'The House of the Rising Sun.'" 2024. https://galaxymusicnotes.com.

Ghost City Tours. "The Ghosts of the Dauphine Orleans Hotel." 2023. https://ghostcitytours.com.

———. "The Ghosts of the Hotel Villa Convento." 2023. https://ghostcitytours.com.

———. "The Ghosts of the St. Pierre Hotel." 2014. https://ghostcitytours.com.

———. "The Haunted Andrew Jackson Hotel." 2016. https://ghostcitytours.com.

———. "The Haunted Bourbon Orleans Hotel." 2019. https://ghostcitytours.com.

Hall, Christie Matherne. "The Saffron Scourge in New Orleans." *Country Roads Magazine*, March 23, 2018. https://countryroadsmagazine.com.

Historic New Orleans Collection Quarterly. "The Ursulines: New Perspectives on 275 Years in New Orleans." Vol. 20, no. 3 (Summer 2002). https://www.hnoc.org.

History.com Editors. "Hurricane Katrina." History.com. https://www.history.com.

Hotel Monteleone. "Hotel Monteleone's Haunted History." June 14, 2024. https://hotelmonteleone.com

Hotel St. Pierre. "About Hotel St. Pierre." 2020. https://www.hotelstpierre.com.

Huddleston, Tom, Jr. "How 4 College Students Tried to Steal Rare Books Worth Millions from a School Library—and What Got Them Caught." CNBC, August 15, 2021. https://www.cnbc.com.

Jan. "Bessie Haynie Brown (1885–1963)." Find a Grave, September 10, 2010. https://www.findagrave.com.

———. "George Walter Brown (1884–1945)." Find a Grave, September 13, 2010. https://www.findagrave.com.

Jannette. "The Haunting History of the Hotel Monteleone." Haunting History Traveling, August 26, 2023. https://huantinghistorytraveling.com.

Kelly, Meghan B. "The Axe Murderer Who Loved Jazz." WBUR, June 22, 2018. https://www.wbur.org.

Kent, Leland. "Lafon Home for Boys." Abandoned Southeast, May 30, 2019. https://abandonedsoutheast.com.

Kingman, William A. "The Axeman of New Orleans." SerialKillerCalendar.com, 2024. https://serialkillercalendar.com.

Kingsley, Karen. "Laura Plantation." 64 Parishes, April 21, 2016. https://64parishes.org.

Kuhn, Laura. "Wandering Spirits of the Dauphine Orleans Hotel." Midnight Boheme, November 18, 2022. https://www.midnightboheme.com.

Laing, Amanda. Review of the Omni Royal Orleans Hotel. Google Reviews, last modified summer 2023. https://maps.app.goo.gl/Ns86M3pLgknWBrPSA.

Landau, Emily. "Storyville." 64 Parishes, January 27, 2011. https://64parishes.org.

Laura Plantation. "History of the Duparc-Locoul Family." 2024. https://www.lauraplantation.com.

Lemmon, Alfred E. 2013. "Orleans Theatre." 64 Parishes, March 28, 2013. https://64parishes.org.

Liversidge, Ava. "House of the Rising Sun: Clarence Ashley, 1933." Bowdoin Orient, September 16, 2022. https://bowdoinorient.com.

Long, Edith E. "VCSBinder." Collins C. Diboll Vieux Carré Digital Survey, October 6, 1964. https://www.hnoc.org.

Longy School of Music of Bard College. "Eric Hofbauer." September 11, 2024. https://longy.edu.

Marshall, Matt. "A Brief History of the 'House of the Rising Sun.'" American Blues Scene, November 20, 2011. https://www.americanbluesscene.com.

Moore, Alahna. "The Rising Sun Hotel." Edited by Charlotte Willcox. New Orleans Historical. https://neworleanshistorical.org.

Mroch, Courtney. "The Ghost That Haunts Hotel Monteleone's Missing 13th Floor." Haunt Jaunts, May 13, 2011. https://www.hauntjaunts.net.

Naked History. "The Great New Orleans Fires of 1788 & 1794." February 23, 2016. https://www.historynaked.com.

Napoleon, Chelsey Richard. "Sisters of the Holy Family." Clerk of Civil District Court Notarial Archives Research Center Blog, December 21, 2021. https://clerkofcivildistrictcourtnotarialarchives.wordpress.com.

National Park Service. "Place d'Armes (Jackson Square)." 2015. https://www.nps.gov.

Nettleton, Mary Anglin, and D. Halle. "Marie Ann Bienvenu Olivier (1772–1843)." Find a Grave, October 11, 2012. https://www.findagrave.com.

———. "Nicholas Goderoy Olivier (1757–1815)." Find a Grave, October 11, 2012. https://www.findagrave.com.

New Orleans Historical. "Old Federal Court House, Before 1895." 2013. https://neworleanshistorical.org.

New Orleans Item. "N.O. Novelist Dives to Her Death from Hotel." Undated clipping.

New Orleans States-Item. "Artist-Poet Found Dead in Bathtub." October 25, 1968.

NewOrleans.com. "Andrew Jackson Hotel." 2024. https://www.neworleans.com.

———. "French Quarter Neighborhood." 2017. https://www.neworleans.com.

Olivier House Hotel. "History." April 23, 2016. https://olivierhouse.com.

———. "New Orleans, Louisiana." 2024. https://www.omnihotels.com.

Omni Hotels & Resorts. "Omni Royal Hotel New Orleans History." 2024. https://www.omnihotels.com.

Oswell, Paul. *New Orleans Historic Hotels*. History Press Library Editions, 2014.

Owens, Kurt. "New Video Shows How the Fires of 1788 and 1794 Changed New Orleans." Historic New Orleans Collection, November 10, 2022. https://www.hnoc.org.

Paranormal New Orleans. "Paranormal New Orleans Episode 3: The Axeman of New Orleans." YouTube, January 2, 2021. https://youtu.be/S4dKYCM78Ds.

Place D'Armes. "History of the Place d'Armes Hotel." August 2023. https://www.placedarmes.com.

Pontchartrain, Blake. "Before the Omni Royal Orleans Hotel, the Hotel Royal Hosted French Quarter Visitors." NOLA.com, August 31, 2024. https://www.nola.com.

———. "Blakeview: The Hotel Monteleone's Famed Carousel Bar Started Spinning 75 Years Ago." NOLA.com, August 31, 2024. https://www.nola.com.

Rose, Alan. *Offbeat New Orleans*. Independently published, 2023.

Rossen, Jake. "The 'Ax Man': New Orleans' Jazz-Loving Serial Killer." Mental Floss, September 12, 2021. https://www.mentalfloss.com.

Saxon, Lyle. Letter to Miss Marge. St. Charles Hotel, New Orleans, Louisiana, October 29, 1942. New Orleans Historical. https://neworleanshistorical.org/files/show/3971.

Scott, Mike. "1839 Olivier Mansion on Toulouse St. Survives Fire, Civil War and Plan to Become a Parking Lot." NOLA.com, November 4, 2021. https://www.nola.com.

———. "A Tale of Destruction, Death, and Maybe a Haunting—at What's Now the Bourbon Orleans Hotel." NOLA.com, October 18, 2021. https://www.nola.com.

———. "200-Year-Old French Quarter Building Has Been a Storied Ballroom, a Historic School and a Swanky Hotel." NOLA.com, December 11, 2019. https://www.nola.com.

Serena, Katie. "The Grisly Crimes of the Axeman of New Orleans, the Vicious Serial Killer Who Targeted Italian Grocers." Edited by Maggie Donahue. All That's Interesting, November 23, 2017. https://allthatsinteresting.com.

Silverman, Emily. "The St. Louis Exchange Hotel and the New Orleans Slave Trade." ViaNolaVie, December 13, 2017. https://www.vianolavie.org.

Smith, Kalila. "Chefs and Cannibals: 'Over the Edge' from *Tales from the French Quarter* by Kalila Smith." Crime Museum, January 24, 2014. https://www.crimemuseum.org.

Soltis, Andy. "Gal-Cooker in an 11-Day 'Stew'por—Confessed in Suicide Note." *New York Post*, October 20, 2006.

Steckler, Melissa, and Liesbeth Ramirez. "Hotel Monteleone." Edited by Kathryn O'Dwyer. New Orleans Historical, March 28, 2016. https://neworleanshistorical.org.

———. "Hotel Monteleone." ViaNolaVie, April 27, 2012. https://www.vianolavie.org.

Succession of Wolf, 17 So.2d 495, 497 (June 26, 1944). Accessed via CaseMine. https://www.casemine.com/judgement/us/5914cb5dadd7b04934801d2d.

Swackhamer, Barry. "Site of First Louisiana School Historical Marker." Edited by Craig Swain. Historical Marker Database, February 12, 2023. https://www.hmdb.org.

Taylor, Micki. "Notes for Unsolved: Dauphine Orleans." BuzzFeed, October 10, 2017. https://www.buzzfeed.com.

Taylor, Troy. *Haunted New Orleans: History & Hauntings of the Crescent City.* The History Press, 2011.

Thomas, Jabari. "One of the Most Haunted Hotels in New Orleans Gets a Frequent Visitor." WGNO, October 20, 2015. https://wgno.com.

Times-Picayune (New Orleans, LA). "Crossbeam Motel Opened in Quarter." November 27, 1969.

———. "Group Attacks Plan for Motel." November 23, 1963.

Todd, Brett, and Kate Mason. "St. Louis Hotel & Exchange: Auctioning off Lives." Edited by Kathryn O'Dwyer. New Orleans Historical, last updated September 21, 2023. https://neworleanshistorical.org.

True Crime Central. "The Case of Addie Hall." YouTube, December 6, 2022. https://youtu.be/Ale1yZRyM7o.

Tyler, Presley Bo. "Louisiana Hotel Ranks on USA Today Reader's Choice List of Top 10 Best Haunted Hotels." *Lafayette Daily Advertiser*, October 28, 2024.

Uitti, Jacob. "Who Is the Writer Behind 'House of the Rising Sun'?" American Songwriter, January 16, 2023. https://americansongwriter.com.

United States District Court, Eastern District of Louisiana. "1812–1823: Historic Federal Courthouses in New Orleans." 2024. https://www.laed.uscourts.gov.

UnXplained Zone. "My Ghost Story: Guests of Haunted Hotel Believe Late Owner's Spirit Is Still Present." YouTube, April 27, 2022. https://youtu.be/SWk_zJA79Xs.

Valentino Hotels New Orleans. https://www.valentinohotels.com.

Various Contributors. "The Axeman of New Orleans." Criminal Minds Wiki, 2024. https://criminalminds.fandom.com.

Very Local. "Is the Olivier House Hotel in New Orleans Haunted?" YouTube, October 20, 2021. https://youtu.be/johGwQHqB0A.

Voltz, Noël M. "Black Female Agency and Sexual Exploitation: Quadroon Balls and Plaçage Relationships." Ohio State University, June 2008. https://kb.osu.edu.

Wegmann, Mary Ann, Law Library of Louisiana and University of New Orleans History Department. "Battle of New Orleans: Old Ursuline Convent." New Orleans Historical, May 13, 2014. https://neworleanshistorical.org.

Wegmann, Mary Ann, Law Library of Louisiana, University of New Orleans History Department and Louisiana State Museum. "The Old Federal Courthouse: Present Day Andrew Jackson Hotel." New Orleans Historical, September 16, 2013. https://neworleanshistorical.org.

Wiese, Jason. "From a Soldier's Stomping Ground to Tourist Attraction: A Brief History of Jackson Square." Historic New Orleans Collection, August 5, 2021. https://www.hnoc.org.

Wikipedia. "The House of the Rising Sun." https://en.wikipedia.

Willoughby, Urmi Engineer. *Yellow Fever, Race, and Ecology in Nineteenth-Century New Orleans.* LSU Press, 2017.

Wolfe, Poet. "A Jazz-Loving, Sadistic Serial Killer Called Axman Terrorized New Orleans. Then He Disappeared." NOLA.com, August 3, 2024. https://www.nola.com.

Wood, Derek. "The Monteleone's Literary Legacy." New Orleans Historical, December 17, 2015. https://neworleanshistorical.org.

Wright, Jade. "Songs from Number One on This Day in History: The House of the Rising Sun and Sunny Afternoon - Liverpool Echo." Liverpool Echo, July 10, 2010. https://www.liverpoolecho.co.uk.

Wulf, Karin. "How Yellow Fever Intensified Racial Inequality in 19th-Century New Orleans." *Smithsonian Magazine*, April 19, 2022. www.smithsonianmag.com.

About the Author

Copyright Amy Shabluk.

Nicole Beauchamp is a world-renowned paranormal researcher from Bay City, Michigan. She holds a bachelor's degree in applied science from Siena Heights University in Adrian, Michigan. In addition to being an author, she also works as a licensed massage therapist. With a lifelong passion for the paranormal and history, Nicole founded the Tri-City Ghost Hunters Society in 2009, after her very first visit to New Orleans. Since forming the group, she has investigated all over the world. Her writing and paranormal journey have been featured in many national and international publications, including *That's Life* magazine, published in Australia and New Zealand; the *Belfast Telegraph*, the leading newspaper in Northern Ireland; and *Sunday World*, the second-largest-selling tabloid-style newspaper in the Republic of Ireland. In 2015, she moved to the Gulf Coast and spent almost four years heavily researching the history and paranormal phenomena of her favorite city, New Orleans. That same year, she wrote a guest editorial for *TAPS Paramagazine* and was featured on *Beyond Reality Radio*, where she was recognized for her hard work and dedication to the paranormal by Jason Hawes, the star of the popular television shows *Ghost Nation* and *Ghost Hunters*. In 2018, Nicole had to move back to Michigan but garnered the nickname "the local who is not a local" from New Orleanians for the sheer amount of time she has spent and continues to spend in the Crescent City. In February 2019, she was featured on the cover of *Paranormal Underground* magazine. She received a tribute from the State of Michigan for her first book, *Haunted Bay City Michigan*, which was released in September 2020. She released her second book, *Haunted Detroit*, in August 2022 and her third, *Haunted Bars & Pubs of Michigan*, in August 2023. She is beyond delighted that her fourth publication is *Haunted French Quarter Hotels*. In addition to the paranormal, she loves traveling and animals. She hopes to continue to tour the country and the world in order to enlighten individuals about the spirit realm. Follow Nicole on Facebook and Instagram: @authornicolebeauchamp

Also by Nicole Beauchamp

Haunted Bars & Pubs of Michigan

Haunted Bay City, Michigan

Haunted Detroit

Visit us at
www.historypress.com